MW01043547

Maurice Sendak

WHO
WROTE
THAT?

Maurice Sendak

Hal Marcovitz

Foreword by
Kyle Zimmer

CHELSEA HOUSE
PUBLISHERS
An imprint of Infobase Publishing

Maurice Sendak

Chelsea House
An imprint of Infobase Publishing
132 West 31st Street
New York NY 10001

Library of Congress Cataloging-in-Publication Data
Marcovitz, Hal.
  Maurice Sendak / Hal Marcovitz.
    p. cm.—(Who wrote that?)
  Includes bibliographical references and index.
  ISBN 0-7910-8796-4
  1. Sendak, Maurice—Juvenile literature. 2. Authors, American—20th
century—Biography—Juvenile literature. 3. Children's stories—Authorship—Juvenile
literature. 4. Illustrators—United States—Biography—Juvenile literature.
I. Title. II. Series.
  PS3569.E6Z76 2006   2005031615
  813'.54aB—dc22

Table of Contents

FOREWORD BY
KYLE ZIMMER
PRESIDENT, FIRST BOOK

HUMANITY IS POWERED by stories. From our earliest days as thinking beings, we employed every available tool to tell each other stories. We danced, drew pictures on the walls of our caves, spoke, and sang. All of this extraordinary effort was designed to entertain, recount the news of the day, explain natural occurrences—and then gradually to build religious and cultural traditions and establish the common bonds and continuity that eventually formed civilizations. Stories are the most powerful force in the universe; they are the primary element that has distinguished our evolutionary path.

Our love of the story has not diminished with time. Enormous segments of societies are devoted to the art of storytelling. Book sales in the United States alone topped $26 billion last year; movie studios spend fortunes to create and promote stories; and the news industry is more pervasive in its presence than ever before.

There is no mystery to our fascination. Great stories are magic. They can introduce us to new cultures, or remind us of the nobility and failures of our own, inspire us to greatness or scare us to death; but above all, stories provide human insight on a level that is unavailable through any other source. In fact, stories connect each of us to the rest of humanity not just in our own time, but also throughout history.

This special magic of books is the greatest treasure that we can hand down from generation to generation. In fact, that spark in a child that comes from books became the motivation for the creation of my organization, First Book, a national literacy program with a simple mission: to provide new books to the most disadvantaged children. At present, First Book has been at work in hundreds of communities for over a decade. Every year children in need receive millions of books through our organization and millions more are provided through dedicated literacy institutions across the United States and around the world. In addition, groups of people dedicate themselves tirelessly to working with children to share reading and stories in every imaginable setting from schools to the streets. Of course, this Herculean effort serves many important goals. Literacy translates to productivity and employability in life and many other valid and even essential elements. But at the heart of this movement are people who love stories, love to read, and want desperately to ensure that no one misses the wonderful possibilities that reading provides.

When thinking about the importance of books, there is an overwhelming urge to cite the literary devotion of great minds. Some have written of the magnitude of the importance of literature. Amy Lowell, an American poet, captured the concept when she said, "Books are more than books. They are the life, the very heart and core of ages past, the reason why men lived and worked and died, the essence and quintessence of their lives." Others have spoken of their personal obsession with books, as in Thomas Jefferson's simple statement: "I live for books." But more compelling, perhaps, is the almost instinctive excitement in children for books and stories.

Throughout my years at First Book, I have heard truly extraordinary stories about the power of books in the lives of children. In one case, a homeless child, who had been bounced from one location to another, later resurfaced—and the only possession that he had fought to keep was the book he was given as part of a First Book distribution months earlier. More recently, I met a child who, upon receiving the book he wanted, flashed a big smile and said, "This is my big chance!" These snapshots reveal the true power of books and stories to give hope and change lives.

As these children grow up and continue to develop their love of reading, they will owe a profound debt to those volunteers who reached out to them—a debt that they may repay by reaching out to spark the next generation of readers. But there is a greater debt owed by all of us—a debt to the storytellers, the authors, who have bound us together, inspired our leaders, fueled our civilizations, and helped us put our children to sleep with their heads full of images and ideas.

Who Wrote That? is a series of books dedicated to introducing us to a few of these incredible individuals. While we have almost always honored stories, we have not uniformly honored storytellers. In fact, some of the most important authors have toiled in complete obscurity throughout their lives or have been openly persecuted for the uncomfortable truths that they have laid before us. When confronted with the magnitude of their written work or perhaps the daily grind of our own, we can forget that writers are people. They struggle through the same daily indignities and dental appointments, and they experience the intense joy and bottomless despair that many of us do. Yet somehow they rise above it all to deliver a powerful thread that connects us all. It is a rare honor to have the opportunity that these books provide to share the lives of these extraordinary people. Enjoy.

Rodeo Drive, a glamorous strip of some of the most expensive stores in Beverly Hills, California, is often portrayed in movies as it is seen here: beautifully lit and always busy. However, during his 1990 visit to Los Angeles, Maurice Sendak found that the movies did not show a realistic view of the street. It was here that he saw a young homeless person sleeping in a box, feet sticking out, and it was from this image that he wrote We Are All in the Dumps With Jack and Guy *(1993).*

1

Confronting the Dark Corners of Childhood

BY 1990, MAURICE SENDAK HAD ALL but decided to give up writing and illustrating children's storybooks. As an illustrator, Sendak had provided art for dozens of storybooks written by some of the world's best-known authors of young people's literature. He had also written many successful storybooks himself, including some of the best-selling children's books of the 1960s, 1970s, and 1980s.

Now, though, Sendak was in search of new challenges. Having been a fan of classical music for a long time, Sendak believed he had found a new direction for his career: designing costumes and sets for opera and ballet productions. Some of his work included designs for the opera *The Magic Flute* by Wolfgang Amadeus Mozart and the ballet *The Nutcracker* by Pyotr Ilyich Tchaikovsky. Sendak had also designed sets and costumes for two musical productions based on his own books *Where the Wild Things Are* and *Really Rosie*. He hoped to begin helping young illustrators get their starts in book publishing. "I needed to be around people," Sendak said in an interview with a news reporter. "I wanted to mentor young artists, to help train them as I had been trained."[1]

In 1990, Sendak traveled to the Los Angeles, California, area to start a new project—designing costumes and sets for Mozart's opera *Idomeneo*. One night, Sendak drove down Rodeo (pronounced ro-DAY-o) Drive, the most exclusive street in the very wealthy neighborhood of Beverly Hills. (Rodeo Drive is lined with stores that sell some of the world's most expensive clothing, furs, and jewelry.) But while driving along Rodeo Drive, Sendak was stunned by what he saw: a young homeless person sleeping in a box, bare feet sticking out. In an interview on National Public Radio he said:

> It was past midnight and we were in a car and we [were] in Beverly Hills, driving and on one of those incredibly unreal, posh L.A. streets there was a dilapidated box with two dirty naked feet sticking out—definitely live feet. I didn't know they belonged to a man, woman, boy, girl. But they looked small enough to be a child's. And just the contradiction of. . . and the juxtaposition of that box, feet and street was alarming—not to say the least, striking. And [it] really kind of ignited the old "We are all in the dumps" verse because suddenly it became apparent to me over a period of days that "dumps" was now. "Dumps" was L.A. and "dumps" was, probably, the world.[2]

After seeing Maurice Sendak's adaptation of his book, **Where the Wild Things Are,** *to opera, the Houston Grand Opera asked if he would design the costumes and sets for their production of* **The Magic Flute,** *written by Sendak's favorite composer, Wolfgang Amadeus Mozart. The scene above shows the two characters from* **The Magic Flute,** *Tamino and Pamina, and the flute itself.*

BASED ON MOTHER GOOSE

That grim scene as well as the words "We are all in the dumps" remained in Sendak's mind. He recalled that the words were part of an old Mother Goose rhyme he had read many years before:

> We are all in the dumps
> For diamonds or trumps
> The kittens are gone to St. Paul's!
> The baby is bit

The moon's in a fit
And the houses are built without walls.[3]

A second rhyme also came to mind:

Jack and Guy went out in the rye
And they found a little boy with one black eye.[4]

Soon, he realized the two rhymes would fit perfectly into a storybook that would tell the tale of the person he had seen sleeping in the box on Rodeo Drive.

In Sendak's version, a little homeless boy, not much older than a baby, is living in a trash dump. The boy and some kittens, who are also living in the dump, are stolen by two evil rats. Two boys, Jack and Guy, walk into the dump and play cards with the evil rats, who cheat them. At first Jack and Guy react coldly to the plight of the boy, but then they decide to rescue him and the kittens.

Sendak finished his work on *Idomeneo*, then he got down to writing and illustrating his story. He worked on *We Are All in the Dumps With Jack and Guy* for two years, finally publishing the storybook in 1993. In the book, Sendak combines the two Mother Goose rhymes to take the reader from the dump, to the ordeal with the rats, and finally, to the rescue in a field of rye. *We Are All in the Dumps With Jack and Guy* is only 114 words long.

The book certainly relates a dark picture to children who perhaps are hearing Sendak's story at bedtime from their parents or are just beginning to read themselves. When asked about the subject matter, Sendak said he is aware that homelessness is not an easy concept for young children to grasp.

GRIM SCENES OF THE CITY

The images Sendak provided for *We Are All in the Dumps With Jack and Guy* are quite harsh. The homeless boy and the other homeless children who live in the dump wear rags

---

Did you know...

Maurice Sendak believes his work as a writer and artist has been inspired by Herman Melville, the 19th-century author whose books were dismissed by critics before they were finally recognized as important contributions to American literature. Melville's best-known work is *Moby-Dick*, the story of the doomed voyage of the New England whaling ship *Pequod* in search of a giant white whale.

"Herman Melville is a god," Sendak told interviewer Bill Moyers in 2004. "I cherish what he did. He was a genius." Sendak said he is particularly taken with Melville's book *Billy Budd*, the story of a young and innocent sailor who earns the hatred of a ship's officer, Claggart, who fears Billy Budd's goodness. "Claggart has him killed in that book," said Sendak. "Claggart has his eye on that boy. He will not tolerate such goodness . . . Goodness is scary."

Sendak has paid tribute to Melville in many of his storybooks. In his book *Swine Lake*, Sendak features an advertisement for Melville's novel *Pierre* in the window of a bookstore. In his storybook *Chicken Soup With Rice*, the child narrator recites the verse: *In November's . . . gusty gale . . . I will flop . . . my flippy tale . . . and spout hot soup! . . . I'll be a whale!* In Moby-Dick, the character Ishmael begins the story by saying he knew it was time to go to sea "whenever there is a damp and drizzly November" in his soul.

for clothes. Many of them live in empty boxes with the words "Biscuits" or "Frozen Food" stamped on the outside. (The boxes at one time held food but by the time the homeless children found them all the food had been eaten by others.) To keep themselves warm at night, the children cover themselves with newspapers carrying advertisements for expensive homes. Sendak centers the story in New York City—there are many familiar landmarks in the book, such as the Brooklyn Bridge and Trump Tower, an exclusive New York skyscraper where the apartments are among the most expensive in the city. Sendak also includes the scene of the young boy's bare feet sticking out of a box he uses for shelter—just as Sendak saw on Rodeo Drive. He said:

> Well, I know it's a very sad subject but I have to tell you I was thrilled to bits to come up with a visualization—finally, after all these years, for these verses. One, it was apropos of the situation in the world today. Two, it touched on my obsession about children and how do children survive—not only just homeless children but middle class children and elitist children. I mean, just children surviving childhood is my obsessive theme and my life's concern.[5]

Over the years, Sendak has heard a lot of criticism about his work. He often tackles tough emotional issues faced by children—such as anger, guilt, loneliness, and fear—and some critics have said young children are not ready for the stories Sendak has decided to tell them. They worried that Sendak's stark images of reality will scare young children— a common complaint that Sendak has endured throughout his career as a writer and illustrator.

We Are All in the Dumps With Jack and Guy was singled out for some particularly biting criticism. In a *New York Times Book Review*, critic Brian Alderson wrote:

Certainly, children are as quick at do-it-yourself deconstruction as the rest of us, and they will find their own stories to tell . . . but I would not force them to it. Guilt, pain and deprivation will be their lot soon enough, and I am not one . . . for giving them an eyeful before their time.[6]

Time magazine, while generally praising the book as "brilliant and powerful stuff"[7] nevertheless cautioned: "it is hard to imagine reading it to a child."[8]

As for Sendak, he believes his books simply tell the truth about childhood. As he told National Public Radio:

I never think childhood is sugar and spice. It's odious and contemptible to say that about childhood and it's such a put-down. Now, of course, childhood is wonderful—let's all say it's wonderful and clap our hands, but then let's say that there are dark corners and alley ways and shadows which are [and] mustn't be ignored.[9]

Maurice Sendak worked part time in high school at All-American Comics where he drew backgrounds for stories that featured Mutt and Jeff, *an enormously popular comic strip of the era created by cartoonist Harry "Bud" Fisher, pictured here. For the most part Sendak drew houses, trees, or puffs of dust to indicate characters' quick getaways.*

2

Evolution of an Artist and Storyteller

WHEN MAURICE SENDAK WAS BORN in Brooklyn, on June 10, 1928, it was a crowded and lively borough of New York City, populated by immigrant families who had left Europe to escape poverty, famine, war, and religious persecution. Maurice's parents, Sarah and Philip Sendak, were Jews from Poland. They arrived in America shortly before World War I, leaving their homes near Warsaw because opportunities for Jews were limited in a society where anti-Semitism (hostility toward or prejudice against Jews and Judaism) was often a way of life.

Sarah and Philip did not know one another before moving to

America. They arrived separately and met while each was trying to start a new life in New York. They married and Philip found work as a dressmaker. He soon shared owner-ship of a tailor shop. Maurice was the youngest of the three Sendak children. When Maurice was born, his brother Jack was 5 years old and his sister Natalie was 9.

As a child, Maurice suffered from many illnesses— measles, pneumonia, and scarlet fever, to name a few. Today, there are vaccines and drugs available to prevent and treat those illnesses, but in the 1920s and 1930s children often had to endure weeks of bed rest to recover from sickness. Each time he got sick, the frail Maurice spent many weeks cooped up in his parents' tiny apartment, battling his symp-toms.

To help his son pass the time, his father would often sit at his bedside and tell stories. Many of the stories were decid-edly scary, drawn from such Jewish mythological creatures as the golem, a living statue with magical powers, or the evil spirit known as Ashmedai, king of the demons. Sometimes, Philip made up the stories, using characters and creatures of his own creation. Whatever the origin of the tales, little Mau-rice was captivated and listened to his father's every word. Later, Sendak recalled, "During my childhood, which seemed like one long series of illnesses, he [Philip] invented beautiful imaginative tales to tell me and my brother and sis-ter. He was a marvelous improviser and would often extend a story for several nights."[10] In an interview on National Public Radio, Sendak recalled one of his father's scariest stories:

> You want an example of why I have been an insomniac all
> my life? Here's a story. It's one of my favorites. I wanted to
> hear it over and over again. The children of his [village] got
> together and as a contest, just the boys [wanted to see] who

could run furthest into the cemetery in the middle of the night. And how do you prove you ran furthest? Because you had a stick, and you would put the stick down, and in the morning you would find out whose stick went the furthest. And he was doing this with his friend and they all ran a certain distance and they couldn't see each other. And he heard this horrible screaming from one of his friends. Horrible screaming. And instead of going to help him, they all ran home. And in the morning they found him dead. And what he had done—because they wore these long shifts—he put the stick in and it went through his own shift. And it went into the ground and he thought the dead man was pulling him in. And his screams were all, "The dead man is taking me! The dead man is taking me!" and they thought he was just hysterical. He thought somebody had reached in and was pulling him into the grave. That was one of his stories—my favorite, actually.[11]

But not all of Philip's stories were scary. Many of the stories included angels. In fact, during one of Maurice's illnesses, his father told him that if he stared hard enough through the window Maurice might be lucky enough to see an angel flying by. If the boy did see the angel, Philip said, it would mean that the illness would be short and Maurice would recover quickly. "But, if you blink, you'll miss it," his father said.[12]

After his father left the room, Maurice stared out the window as hard as he could. Suddenly, he shouted, "I saw it, I saw it!"[13] His father rushed back in the room. When Philip asked his son what all the excitement was about, Maurice told his father that he saw an angel. Philip was delighted to hear the news. "He was as thrilled as I was," Sendak recalled.[14]

PINKY, MICKEY, AND MUTT

The Sendak family moved often during Maurice's child-hood. Sarah Sendak could not tolerate the odor of fresh paint. This meant that every time their landlord wanted to repaint the apartments in his building, the Sendak family would move out. And so, Maurice's childhood was spent moving from apartment to apartment. He would have to make new friends whenever the family settled into a new home but since he was sickly, Maurice found it hard to make friends. It was difficult for him to learn the games played by young children on the Brooklyn streets when he was struck in bed. He also stuttered, which added to his shyness. Sendak recalled:

> I was a miserable kid. I couldn't make friends. I couldn't skate great, I couldn't play stoopball terrific . . . You know what they all thought of me: sissy Maurice Sendak. Whenever I wanted to go out and do something, my father would say, "You'll catch cold." And I did. I did whatever he told me.[15]

Sitting at the window of his apartment, watching the other children play games in the street below, Sendak started developing his talent as an artist. He spent hours sketching the street scenes he saw below his window. One of his favorite subjects was a girl from the neighborhood named Rosie. "She was about three years younger than me, so we were not in the same circle of friends," said Sendak. "We never spoke on the street or made eye contact. But she was a grand performer who would dress up in costumes from her mother's wardrobe and improvise shows for the neighbor-hood children."[16] In later years, Rosie would emerge as a character featured prominently in Sendak's work as a story-book writer and artist.

Sendak is largely a self-taught artist. Although as a young adult he attended art classes at night, as a boy he received little training in art during elementary or high school. Indeed, at Lafayette High School in Brooklyn, Sendak's art teacher conducted most of the lessons by setting up a still life in front of the class—a bowl of fruit, for example, or a vase of flowers—and then leaving the students on their own to sketch or paint.

By high school, Sendak had shaken off the childhood illnesses that had plagued his younger years. Soon, he emerged as the best artist at Lafayette High School, providing illustrations for the school yearbook, literary magazine, and student newspaper, the *Lafayette News*. In fact, for the newspaper he created his own comic strip, titled *Pinky Carrd*, which followed the antics of a dimwitted student who bumbled his way through Lafayette High School.

Since the age of 6, Sendak has been a movie fan. The Sendak family visited the neighborhood theater every week so that Sarah could collect the free dinner plates the theater owner gave away as a promotion; nevertheless, the Friday night trip to the movies was often the only time Maurice could spend outside the apartment. His favorite part of the experience was the cartoon shown before the main feature. Usually, the cartoon was produced by the studio of Walt Disney, the creator of Mickey Mouse. Later, Natalie, Jack, and Maurice rode the subway into Manhattan, New York's business and entertainment district, to see movies at Radio City Music Hall—the city's grandest theater. Among the movies Maurice saw as a young boy were the full-length Disney animations *Snow White*, *Pinocchio*, and *Fantasia*. As a child, Maurice developed an intense admiration for Disney's work.

While in high school Sendak found a part-time job with

Did you know...

The first book Maurice Sendak recalls reading as a young boy was *The Prince and the Pauper*, Mark Twain's story of intrigue and adventure in 16th-century England when a prince and a poor boy change places as part of a game. In a 1972 interview with Virginia Haviland, head of the children's book section at the Library of Congress, Sendak recalled that he treated the book as more than just an object to read, and that he believes most young children regard books as he did—as important additions to their lives. He said:

> My sister bought me my first book, *The Prince and the Pauper* . . . The first thing was to set it up on the table and stare at it for a long time. Not because I was impressed with Mark Twain; it was just such a beautiful object. Then came the smelling of it . . . *The Prince and the Pauper* smelled good and it also had a shiny cover, a laminated cover. I flipped over that. And it was very solid. I mean, it was bound very tightly. I remember trying to bite into it, which I don't imagine is what my sister intended when she bought the book for me. But the last thing I did with the book was read it. It was all right. But I think it started then, a passion for books and bookmaking. I wanted to be an illustrator very early in my life; to be involved in books in some way—to make books . . . I've seen children touch books, fondle books, smell books, and it's all the reason in the world why books should be beautifully produced.

All-American Comics, a publisher that produced comic book-length stories featuring the characters found on the funny pages of the daily and Sunday newspapers. Sendak was assigned to draw the backgrounds for the stories that featured *Mutt and Jeff*, an enormously popular comic strip of the era created by cartoonist Harry "Bud" Fisher. The very tall Mutt and the very short Jeff were best friends who liked to stay out late playing cards, betting on horses at the track, or concocting get-rich-quick schemes—antics that often found Mutt in trouble with his wife, the very ill-tempered Mrs. Mutt. Sendak's job was to draw houses or trees in the backgrounds of the comic strip panels, or to draw a puff of dust to indicate the "poof" made by a character suddenly running away—usually Mutt, attempting to flee the rolling pin-wielding Mrs. Mutt.

WINDOW DESIGNER

Maurice graduated from Lafayette High School in 1946. College was out of the question—Philip Sendak had lost all of his money in the Wall Street crash of 1929 and the Sendak family never recovered. Philip and Sarah could not afford college for their children.

Instead, Maurice found a job working for Timely Service, a company that decorated window displays for New York's department stores. During the era, and certainly still today, department stores in cities invested in very elaborate displays in their windows to show off the fashions, jewelry, or other wares that could be found inside. Displays have always been important because they catch people's eyes and help draw customers into the stores.

Typically, artists are hired to design the displays because they often require a degree of craftsmanship. Sendak recalled one early assignment required him to create a scene featuring life-size figures of Snow White and the seven dwarfs. He fashioned each character in the display out of chicken wire covered with papier-mâché. Sendak said:

> It was one of the best times of my life. I was in Manhattan, I was meeting all kinds of people I never met in Brooklyn. They were people who felt they were really artists and considered their work for Timely Service as just a job that enabled them to paint seriously at night.[17]

While working at Timely Services, Maurice moved out of his parents' apartment and found a place of his own. At night, he took classes in art at a trade school.

He enjoyed his new-found independence but, alas, it would be short-lived. At Timely Service, Sendak received a promotion that required him to design and build window displays in a warehouse off-site, meaning he no longer worked right in the department store windows. Sendak found the new assignment boring and, since most of his co-workers were much older, he made few friends at the new location. And so, in 1948 he quit and moved back in with his parents. "Out of a job, out of sorts, and out of money, and—worse—having to live at home with my parents again," he said.[18]

At home, Sendak passed the time the same way he had done as a sickly child—sitting at the window of his parent's apartment, sketching the scenes of city life below. He found himself drawn to scenes of children at play, and filled many sketchbooks of young people skipping and hop-scotching through the streets. He went back to drawing pictures of "Rosie." Sendak said, "It seems on the evidence of that sketchbook and the ones that came quickly after, that the better part of my day was spent at the window Rosie-watching."[19]

Five years older than Maurice, Jack Sendak had recently

In 1949 Maurice Sendak and his older brother Jack designed a series of mechanical wooden toys based on characters in classic children's stories. They took their prototypes to F.A.O. Schwarz, the big toy store on Fifth Avenue in Manhattan shown above, where they met with a buyer. While F.A.O. Schwarz decided against purchasing the toys, executives offered Sendak a job designing the store's window displays, which eventually got him his first illustrating job: The Wonderful Farm *by Marcel Aymé.*

been discharged from duty in the U.S. Army. Back home in Brooklyn, the two brothers conceived of a way to make money. In 1949 they designed a series of mechanical wooden toys based on storybook scenes found in such classic tales as "Little Miss Muffett," "Little Red Riding Hood," "Hansel and Gretel," "Aladdin's Lamp," "Old Mother Hubbard," and "Pinocchio." The toys were elaborate and painstakingly detailed: Jack did the engineering and woodworking while Maurice painted the figures.

Immensely proud of their work, the brothers took their prototypes to F.A.O. Schwarz, the big toy store on Fifth Avenue in Manhattan, where they met with a buyer. Their plan was to get a commitment from F.A.O. Schwarz to buy hundreds of copies; the brothers would then go into the toy-making business. "We visualized a workshop full of little old men creating the wooden parts, and we would not have permitted any kind of plastic substitute," Maurice said.[20]

The buyer at the store was impressed with the toys but believed they would be too expensive to produce in large quantities for the store to make a profit. But executives at the store saw the talent behind the prototypes and offered Maurice a job designing the store's window displays. Out of work since quitting Timely Services the previous year and with no other prospects, Maurice accepted the offer.

He would not be decorating the toy store's windows for long. F.A.O. Schwarz featured an extensive children's book selection. Maurice found himself spending hours poring over the books he found for sale in the store, absorbing the styles of such famous 19th- and 20th-century illustrators as George Cruikshank, Walter Crane, Randolph Caldecott, Hans Fischer, Felix Hoffmann, and Alois Carigiet. Spending as much time as he did in the children's book department, Maurice became friendly with F.A.O. Schwarz's children's book buyer, who introduced him to Ursula Nordstrom, the children's book editor at the publishing company known then as Harper & Brothers.

One day in 1950, Nordstrom dropped by Maurice's workshop at F.A.O. Schwarz to examine his sketches of Rosie and the other neighborhood children as well the other ideas he had put down on paper in his sketchbook. The next day, she called to offer him an assignment: Harper & Brothers planned to publish a collection of stories by French author Marcel Aymé titled *The Wonderful Farm*. Would he illustrate the book? Maurice accepted immediately. That telephone call would be the beginning of a long and rewarding relationship that would lead to one of the most successful collaborations in the history of children's literature in America.

A Hole is to Dig

Sendak produced a series of whimsical drawings to accompany Aymé's stories. The book was published in 1951. It was not a big seller, but Nordstrom was delighted with Sendak's work and soon gave him another assignment: illustrating a book by author Ruth Krauss titled *A Hole is to Dig*.

In agreeing to publish Krauss's book, Harper & Brothers was taking something of a chance. The book was part of a new trend that had arrived in children's literature in the early 1950s: these new books did not tell stories, instead, they were based on real-life ideas and feelings that originated among children.

Krauss wrote *A Hole is to Dig* after speaking with a number of children and encouraging them to give, in their own words, definitions for common objects and people in their lives. The book contains such definitions as "Dogs are to kiss people," "Hands are to hold," "The world is so you have something to stand on," "Buttons are to keep people warm," and, as the title suggests, "A hole is to dig." Nordstom recalled, "We had already turned down a number of illustrators for the new Ruth Krauss book, *A Hole is to Dig*. We needed something very special, and Maurice's sketchbook made me think he would be perfect for it."[21]

Unlike working on Aymé's book, Sendak worked closely with Krauss to produce the illustrations for *A Hole is to Dig*. He traveled often to Krauss's home in Connecticut, where the author and illustrator spent much time discussing the images that would go on each page. Together, they decided that since the book recalled simple times when simple definitions could sum up matters of enormous complexity, the book should have an old-fashioned, 19th-century feel to it. And so Sendak produced pen and ink drawings on brown-tinted paper. On the page in which the definition of a dog is illustrated, Sendak drew 16 children of various shapes and sizes happily receiving generous licks from their puppies.

Published in 1952, the book was well-received by the children's literature community. The book critic for the *New York Times* declared *A Hole is to Dig* "a unique book."[22] The critic for *Horn Book*, a magazine that reports on young people's literature, wrote, "Entirely original in approach. The illustrations are perfect."[23]

Indeed, *A Hole is to Dig* has remained a very popular book; more than five decades after its publication, the book continues to sell thousands of copies a year. As for Sendak, more than *The Wonderful Farm*, *A Hole is to Dig* would launch him on his career as a storybook illustrator. With the money he earned as a collaborator on Krauss's book, he was able to move out of his parent's apartment and find his own place in Manhattan's Greenwich Village—the neighborhood where, at the time, many of New

York's most successful writers and artists were living. He was also able to give up his window decorating job at F.A.O. Schwarz and devote his efforts full time to illustrating children's storybooks.

LEVELS OF FANTASY

Throughout the 1950s, Sendak found his services as an illustrator very much in demand as he provided drawings for books authored by more than a dozen writers of children's storybooks. Over the next decade, Sendak illustrated eight more books written by Krauss as well as books written by Meindert DeJong (*Hurry Home, Candy*; *Along Came a Dog*; and *The Wheel on the School*), Else Holemelund Minarik (*Little Bear*; *Father Bear Comes Home*; and *Little Bear's Friend*), and Beatrice S. de Regniers (*What Can You Do With a Shoe?* and *The Giant Story*), among others. His brother Jack proved to be a talented writer, and Sendak provided illustrations for two of his brother's storybooks, *Circus Girl* and *The Happy Rain*.

During this period, Sendak often thought of writing and illustrating his own storybook. In 1955, at the age of 27, Sendak read a book authored by the psychologist Dorothy Baruch. The book, *One Little Boy*, was about one of her cases involving a disturbed little boy who did not seem to care about the direction of his life. Sendak drew inspiration from Baruch's book. He took the child examined by Baruch and made him the main character in the first storybook he wrote and illustrated. Even the name was the same. Sendak established Kenny as the type of child who would show up in most of his books—children who "are held back by life, but, one way or another, manage miraculously to find release from their troubles."[24]

Up till that point, Sendak had done very little writing. Although he had penned the stories for his *Pinky Carrd* comic strips back at Lafayette High School, since then he had made few attempts to supply the stories for his artwork. Sendak decided to spend the summer of 1955 at Yelping Hill, a retreat in Connecticut for writers provided on the estate of Henry Seidel Canby, a noted book editor. That summer, Ursula Nordstrom made the trip to Connecticut to help Sendak work out the details of his story. "We would walk in the woods and talk about what I was trying to say," Sendak recalled. "She was endlessly patient and immensely helpful."[25]

The story he created centers on a young boy who wakes from a dream to discover a four-legged rooster demanding answers to seven unusual questions:

> Can you draw a picture on the blackboard when
>   somebody doesn't want you to?
> What is an only goat?
> Can you hear a horse on the roof?
> Can you fix a broken promise?
> What is a very narrow escape?
> What looks inside and what looks outside?
> Do you always want what you think you want?[26]

If Kenny is able to find the answers to these questions, he will be rewarded with a trip to a magical garden where the sun and moon shine in the sky at the same time and he will never have to go to bed.

The book, *Kenny's Window*, takes Kenny on seven adventures as he looks for the answer to each question. On his adventure in search of the "only goat," for example, Kenny rides a train to Switzerland that rumbles up and down the

Swiss Alps; in other adventures, he discusses his mission with his dog and must be kind to his teddy bear, Bucky, whose feelings have been hurt. By the end of the story, Kenny has answered all seven questions but decides not to go to the magic garden. Instead, he chooses to go home.

Sendak said he wanted *Kenny's Window* to show how a child could take control of his own dreams and how children often try to merge a make-believe world with the real world. The combination of real with make-believe would become a common theme in Sendak's books in the years to come. He said:

> Fantasy is so all-pervasive—I don't think there's any part of our lives, as adults or children, when we're not fantasizing, but we prefer to relegate that activity to children, as if fantasy were some tomfoolery only fit for immature minds. Children do not live in both fantasy and reality; they move back and forth with ease, in a way that we no longer remember how to do. And in writing for children I always assume that they have this incredible flexibility, this cool sense of the logic or illogic, and that they can move with me from one sphere to the other without any problems. Fantasy is the core of all writing for children, as I think it is for the writing of any book—perhaps even for the act of living. Certainly, it is crucial to my work. There are many kinds of fantasy and levels of fantasy and subtleties of fantasy—there is probably no such thing as creativity without fantasy.[27]

Kenny's Window was published in 1956. Sendak said that if there is one weakness in the book, it is probably in his illustrations. Sendak does not believe the pen and ink drawings he provided properly illustrated the fantasies in Kenny's life. Looking back, he thinks the drawings could have used a more whimsical approach. He said, "The pictures are ghastly—I really wasn't up to illustrating my own texts then. And the story itself, to be honest, is nice but long-winded."[28]

Sendak followed up *Kenny's Window* with *Very Far Away*, which was published in 1957. In this story, a boy named Martin realizes that his mother is too busy caring for his newborn sibling to pay attention to him. He decides to run away, very far away, and once he is there he finds three friends, a bird, a horse, and a cat, with whom to play and complain. Eventually, however, Martin grows tired of his rebellious adventure and returns home.

The Sign on Rosie's Door, published in 1960, was better received and was the first time Sendak had put the character of Rosie—the girl he sketched on the street below his parents' apartment in Brooklyn when he was growing up—into one of his stories. In *The Sign on Rosie's Door*, Rosie is depicted as Sendak remembered her—a young girl who loved to live in a fantasy world: dressing up and putting on shows for her friends. In the story, Rosie takes the role of a beautiful singer "Alinda," who interrupts the boredom of a summer's day by putting on a show. The book concludes:

> "It's getting late," said Kathy. "I have to go home."
>
> "Wasn't it a wonderful show?" asked Rosie.
>
> "It was the best I ever saw," Kathy answered. "Let's have another one soon."
>
> "Same time, same place," said Rosie.
>
> "Good-by, Cha-Charoo."
>
> "Good-by, Alinda."
>
> Rosie was all alone. She climbed on top of a folding chair

and said very quietly, "Ladies and gentlemen, Alinda will now sing, 'On the Sunny Side of the Street.'"

And she sang the song all the way to the end.[29]

In 1963, Maurice Sendak published Where the Wild Things Are, *now one of his most well known books, and the next year the American Library Association (ALA) awarded* Where the Wild Things Are *the Caldecott Medal. In 1975, Sendak adapted* Where the Wild Things Are *to opera, providing the story and designing the sets and costumes while Oliver Knussen wrote the music. Above is a scene from a 1985 production of their musical creation at the Glyndebourne Festival Theatre.*

3

Three
Important
Books

KENNY'S WINDOW, VERY FAR AWAY, and *The Sign on Rosie's Door* convinced Maurice Sendak that he was able to use words to tell a story, but he was not satisfied with his efforts. He felt the words carried the stories and that the illustrations were weak. He wanted to devise a book in which the illustrations were bold but not overwhelming. He wanted the young reader to enjoy the pictures, but still use the words to follow the storyline. In 1963, he published a storybook that fulfilled his dream: *Where the Wild Things Are*. The book proved to be Sendak's most important work. Indeed, it has been read by millions of young children and their parents and recognized as a milestone in children's literature. And like most of Sendak's books, *Where the Wild Things Are* has sparked controversy over whether it is proper reading material for a young audience.

The story, which is made up of just 338 words, follows the antics of a young boy named Max who dresses in a wolf suit and makes mischief by chasing his dog with a fork. His mother grows angry and calls him a "wild thing." When Max threatens to eat his mother, she sends him to bed without his supper. Entering his bedroom, Max finds that a forest is growing around his bed. Growing denser, the forest thickens "until his ceiling hung with vines and the walls became the world all around."[30]

Next, Max boards a boat, sails across an ocean on a journey that takes him nearly a year, then lands in a place "where the wild things are."[31] He finds huge, scary monsters who try to frighten him, but Max tames the beasts and becomes their king. He then leads them in an all-night party, a "wild rumpus," in which the monsters hop and howl, swing from tree branches, and stomp around the forest until Max finally tires and sends the beasts to bed without supper. In the end, Max decides to leave the wild things and return home, where he finds his supper waiting for him.

Sendak wanted to blend fantasy and reality in the story. Early in the book, as Max chases the dog, he runs by a drawing tacked to the wall. The drawing depicts a monster and is signed "by Max." Sendak also included an illustration of Max creating a homemade tent, fashioned from a bed linen and a string of handkerchiefs tied together. Most young children have made similar play tents, although it is likely they would not use Max's method—knocking a nail into a wall. Still, later in the book Max, as king of the wild things, occupies a grand and luxurious tent. Certainly, there are elements of Max's real word merging with his dream world.

Where the Wild Things Are fulfilled Sendak's dream of providing bold illustrations for a storyline. Unlike the pen and ink drawings used in some of his previous works, Sendak used bright colors to illustrate *Where the Wild Things Are*, applying them in wide strokes. Black ink accentuates the features of the characters. In the book, *The Art of Maurice Sendak*, author Selma G. Lanes commented that the pages featuring the wild rumpus

> . . . probably comprise the best-thumbed pages in contemporary children's literature. In the first, Max and four large wild things dance and bay at the moon. Max, wearing his crown, is clearly a fit "king of all wild things." Inexplicably, a full moon now shines over their merrymaking, but at this enchanted moment no reader will quibble with the artist's lunar license. The second spread—which shifts to morning light—shows Max and his companions swinging companionably, like monkeys, from the familiar trees. In the final spread, Max is mounted triumphantly on the bristly shoulders of the wildest wild thing, and all creatures look ecstatically happy. When Max willingly gives up his crown to sail back home "into the night of his very own room where he found his supper waiting for him," the illustration shows a smiling, spent Max, his wolf hood slipping off his head [a subtle reminder that he has been purged of his wildness and rage]. On the table we see Max's supper, with a large piece of cake for dessert [suggesting that his mother has entirely forgiven him.][32]

WINNING THE CALDECOTT MEDAL

It did not take long for critics to attack *Where the Wild Things Are*. Many critics complained that a children's storybook

Did you know...

Early in his career, Maurice Sendak won the prestigious Caldecott Medal for *Where the Wild Things Are*. The award was named in honor of Randolph Caldecott, a 19th-century British author and illustrator who helped revolutionize storybook art.

Among Caldecott's most famous works are the book *The House that Jack Built*, published in 1878, and the illustrations for books written by the American author Washington Irving. In 1884, a book of nursery rhymes illustrated by Caldecott sold nearly 900,000 copies. Among his admirers were the artists Paul Gaugin and Vincent Van Gogh.

Sendak has long been an admirer of Caldecott's work. He said Caldecott had a gift for making action come alive on a page, often using a single word of text to spark a particularly lively and dramatic scene. Commenting in the 1998 book *A Caldecott Celebration*, Sendak said a Caldecott illustration "gallop[s] full-blast . . . at you."

Caldecott suffered from ill health for most of his life. He spent much of his time traveling, seeking warm climates where he could escape the chill of winters in England. In 1886, Caldecott and his wife Marian traveled to the United States where they hoped to spend the winter in sunny Florida. Unfortunately, it was unseasonably cold that year and Caldecott fell ill and died in St. Augustine, Florida, on February 12, 1886. He was not yet 40 years old. To honor Caldecott, the Caldecott Medal is awarded annually to a children's storybook illustrator by the Association for Library Services to Children, a division of the American Library Association.

was no place to show a child directing anger toward his mother or, from an opposite point of view, a mother punishing her child by sending him to bed without supper. Writing in *Ladies Home Journal*, child psychologist Bruno Bettelheim said Sendak chose an inappropriate way to describe the "destructive fantasies in the child,"[33] adding, "What he failed to understand is the incredible fear it evokes in the child to be sent to bed without supper, and this by the first and foremost giver of food and security—his mother."[34] Critics also wondered whether Max's response to his mother's punishment—his threat to eat her—would spark nightmares in the book's readers. Writing in the *Saturday Review*, critic Alice Dalgliesh suggested *Where the Wild Things Are* "has disturbing possibilities for the child."[35]

Sendak countered, saying that his story shows that children harbor feelings of rage and anger and, like adults, often deal with their feelings by escaping into a fantasy world. He said there is an "inescapable fact of childhood— the awful vulnerability of children and their struggle to make themselves king of all wild things."[36] As for his readers, well, they loved the book. When *New York Times* reporter Saul Braun asked his 6-year-old son Tony what he thought of *Where the Wild Things Are*, the boy exclaimed, "That's my favorite book."[37]

In 1964, *Where the Wild Things Are* was awarded the Caldecott Medal by the American Library Association (ALA). The medal, which honors 19th-century storybook illustrator Randolph Caldecott, is regarded as one of the most prestigious awards in children's literature. The award's presentation to Sendak established him as an important voice in the world of storybook writing and illustration, and it also put aside the criticism that the messages contained in his books are too dark for children to absorb.

One of Sendak's book editors, Michael di Capua, told the *New York Times*:

> *Wild Things* split the establishment. There were people who were horrified when it won the Caldecott. They pinned their objections on the monsters, but they really objected to knowing that children get angry at their mothers. These are the people who tend to sentimentalize childhood, to be overprotective. Maurice has almost single-handedly opened a door on another world.[38]

Since its publication, *Where the Wild Things Are* has remained a staple on the shelves of bookstores and libraries in America and elsewhere. It has been translated into 13 languages and sold more than two million copies. In 2002, *Publisher's Weekly*—a magazine that covers the publishing industry—listed *Where the Wild Things Are* sixty-third on its list of 150 best-selling children's books of all time.

IN THE NIGHT KITCHEN

Following *Where the Wild Things Are*, Sendak provided illustrations for a number of storybooks written by other authors, including an anthology of stories written by Isaac Bashevis Singer, the Polish-American Jewish author and Nobel Prize winner. Sendak particularly enjoyed his work on the Singer book because as a boy his father, Philip Sendak, had often told him Singer's stories. Indeed, Sendak once boasted to his parents that he would one day illustrate Singer's stories—that boast came true in 1966 when he illustrated Singer's *Zlateh the Goat and Other Stories*.

In 1969, Sendak started work on a book that he would regard as his most rewarding project: writing and illustrating a volume he titled *In the Night Kitchen*. The book, which is just 322 words long, tells the story of a little boy named Mickey who wakes up one night to clanging sounds in the kitchen below. Heading downstairs to investigate, he does not find his mother at work in the kitchen, but rather three rotund bakers busily preparing the batter for the next morning's bread. They spot Mickey and mistake him for a jar of milk. Adding Mickey to the mixing bowl, they prepare the batter and, just before they slide it into the oven, Mickey pops out and makes his escape by fashioning an airplane out of bread dough. He flies the plane through the kitchen and then into the Milky Way galaxy to find milk for the recipe. Finally, after delivering the milk, Sendak wrote: "Now Mickey in the night kitchen cried . . . and slid down the side . . . straight into bed . . . cakefree and dried."[39]

Sendak said he wrote the book because most young children have the desire to stay up past their bedtimes to see what goes on in their homes after the lights go out. Many children harbor fantasies about what life is like after the sun goes down, he said, and *In the Night Kitchen* provides one version of just what might be going on downstairs while little boys and girls are asleep.

Sendak said he got the idea for *In the Night Kitchen* after recalling an advertisement for a bakery that boasted its employees worked all night to make bread so that it could be fresh in the morning. In a 1972 interview conducted at the Library of Congress in Washington, Sendak said:

> It seemed to me the most sadistic thing in the world, because all I wanted to do was stay up and watch. And it seemed so absurdly cruel and arbitrary for them to do it while I slept. And also for them to think I would think that was terrific stuff on their part, you know, and would eat their product on top of that.[40]

Mickey was named after Mickey Mouse—the animated Disney character responsible for first sparking Sendak's interest in art. Fans of old-time movies will notice that Sendak fashioned the three bakers to resemble the comedian Oliver Hardy—the bakers are very round and very jovial with tiny mustaches growing beneath bulbous noses. The Night Kitchen is designed to resemble New York City at night—jars of jam and yeast, boxes of cake mix, coconut, cartons of baby formula, and condensed milk are drawn to resemble buildings. Sendak recalled that as a child, when his sister took him to see movies at Radio City Music Hall, she always took him to an elegant New York restaurant for a meal. "Somehow to me New York represented eating," he said.[41]

Librarians fretted because after Mickey rises from bed, he slips out of his pajamas as he descends to the Night Kitchen and spends the rest of the adventure in the nude— a circumstance that would lead to censorship battles over the book. Indeed, the book stirred controversy. Some critics believed Sendak tried to send a quiet message about anti-Semitism in the book. At one point, Mickey is nearly baked in the oven along with the bread. Was this a reference to the Jews who died in Nazi gas ovens during World War II? Also, critics could not help but notice that the bakers employed kosher salt—the box of the large-granuled cooking salt held by one of Sendak's bakers features a six-pointed Jewish star. (The term "kosher" is applied to certain foods that conform with Jewish dietary laws.) Sendak dismissed the complaints and interpretations of his work, insisting that the book was written as nothing more than a tribute to New York City:

> You got dressed up, and you went uptown, and it was night when you got there, and there were lots of windows blinking,

and you went straight to a place to eat. It was one of the most exciting things of my childhood, to do this. Cross the bridge, and see the city approaching, and get there, and have your dinner, and then go to a movie, and come home. So, again *In the Night Kitchen* is a kind of homage to New York City, the city I loved so much and still love. It had a special quality for me as a child.[42]

OUTSIDE OVER THERE

In 1981, Sendak published *Outside Over There*—the third book in what is regarded as the trilogy of his most important works. The 359-word book tells the story of a baby's kidnapping by a group of goblins and the rescue by the baby's older sister, Ida. Sendak said the story was inspired by the kidnapping of the Lindbergh baby in 1932—a story that he admits caused him fears as a young child.

Charles Lindbergh was a pioneer aviator and American hero who, in 1927, became the first pilot to fly solo across the Atlantic Ocean. The feat proved that aviation could be a safe and effective means of transportation, and Lindbergh's flight did a lot to launch aviation into the industry it is today. But Lindbergh's story is also tragic. In 1932, the aviator's 19-month-old son was kidnapped from his family's home in New Jersey. Later, the child was murdered by his abductor. Police arrested a carpenter, Bruno Hauptmann, and charged him with the crime. After a trial that transfixed the nation, Hauptmann was convicted of the abduction and murder and executed.

Sendak was just 4 years old when Hauptmann was put to death, but the kidnapping dominated the news and much was written and broadcast about the crime for years after it occurred. Sendak said he grew up hearing adults talk about the Lindbergh case and quite often found he was fearful of

WANTED

INFORMATION AS TO THE WHEREABOUTS OF

CHAS. A. LINDBERGH, JR.

OF HOPEWELL, N. J.

SON OF COL. CHAS. A. LINDBERGH

World-Famous Aviator

This child was kidnaped from his home in Hopewell, N. J., between 8 and 10 p. m. on Tuesday, March 1, 1932.

DESCRIPTION:

Age, 20 months	Hair, blond, curly
Weight, 27 to 30 lbs.	Eyes, dark blue
Height, 29 inches	Complexion, light

Deep dimple in center of chin
Dressed in one-piece coverall night suit

Maurice Sendak's book Outside Over There, *published in 1981, tells the story of a baby's kidnapping by a group of goblins and the rescue by the baby's older sister, Ida. The story was inspired by the 1932 kidnapping of the world-famous pilot Charles Lindbergh's son, Charles A. Lindbergh Jr. Sendak was 4 years old at the time of the kidnapping, and the story scared him. The poster, shown here, was distributed to police chiefs in more then 1,400 cities across the United States.*

abduction. Those thoughts remained with him for many years and, finally, he decided to write and illustrate a storybook about the abduction of a young child.

Outside Over There follows the adventure of a girl named Ida who must rescue her baby sister from an abduction by goblins. With the children's father away at sea and their mother sitting off by herself "in the arbor," Ida is left alone to look after her sister. As Ida plays her horn, the hooded goblins sneak into the home and abduct the child, fooling Ida by leaving an ice sculpture of the baby behind. When her "sister" begins melting, Ida discovers the abduction and chases after the goblins. Climbing backwards out of the window, Ida falls into a magical world—"outside over there"—where she flies through the sky searching for her sister. She finds the goblins, and after pulling off their hoods discovers they are no more than babies themselves. Playing her horn, she makes them dance into a stream, leaving behind "one who lay cozy in an eggshell, crooning and clapping as a baby should. And that was Ida's sister."[43] Ida and her baby sister return home, where they are reunited with their mother.

In an interview with Roger Sutton, the editor of *Horn Book* magazine, Sendak explained that *Outside Over There* was intended to help children confront their fears.

> *Outside Over There* brought some hostility from children, but it was a book that made them chew. It works; that's all I know. It just works and whatever that means, that's what you've got to do. You've got to make it work. On whatever level, you've got to aim that arrow even though you don't know the target, really, you don't even know why you're so vehement. I hate being this mysterious, but I can't help it because I don't get it; I've never understood this—process,

impulse, intuition, subject matter, what pulls me here and not there, what will unleash an enormous excitement in me while other things that I thought would, don't.[44]

By now, critics of children's literature had come to expect Sendak to offer dark stories that explored turf not ordinarily visited in storybooks. Indeed, few storybooks tell tales of abduction. Unlike *Where the Wild Things Are* and *In the Night Kitchen*, critics found reason to praise Sendak for venturing into unknown territory. Writing in *Newsweek* magazine, book reviewer Walter Clemens said *Outside Over There* includes "fears, rages, and appetites that adults would prefer to believe children don't experience. But *Outside Over There* . . . deals with the more complex feelings of an older child."[45] And in the *New York Times Book Review*, critic John Gardner wrote that *Outside Over There* is "a book for children that treats the child reader as a serious, intelligent, troubled and vulnerable human being . . . Another writer might have softened the tale's effect by humor. Mr. Sendak does something better: By the lyricism and gentle irony of his words and pictures, he transmutes guilt and insecurity—the dual bane of every child's existence—the things one can muse on without undue fear and escape triumphant."[46]

Outside Over There ends with a positive message. In the end, Ida safely delivers her sister back home to the comfort of her mother's arms. All children, Sendak said, and even many adults, including himself, look forward to that type of ending. He said:

I have touched the place where I wanted to go and, when Ida goes home, I go home. No other work of art has given me this inner peace and happiness. I have caught that thing that has eluded me for so long, so critical to living; and knowing that means everything, regardless of what anyone else says about the book, I'm not a happy man. I'm notorious for that. *Outside Over There* made me happy.[47]

Each year, hundreds of books face censorship, and every fall, the American Library Association (ALA) sponsors Banned Books Week to call attention to censorship. They announce a list of the 10 most-challenged titles. In 2004, the list included a classic novel, Of Mice and Men, *written by John Steinbeck, pictured above. Steinbeck's book made the list because of the author's use of offensive language. Maurice Sendak's* In the Night Kitchen *also made the 2004 list because Mickey is naked throughout his adventures.*

4

Drawing Diapers on Mickey

IN 1972, WHEN A STAFF MEMBER at Caldwell Parish Library in Louisiana paged through a copy of *In the Night Kitchen*, she was shocked to find the hero, Mickey, spending much of his adventure without wearing clothes. The librarian believed the image of a little naked boy in the pages of a storybook was not proper reading material for the young children of Caldwell Parish, so she found a jar of white paint and added a little extra art to the book. She painted a diaper on Mickey.

The magazine *School Library Journal* learned of the librarian's deft use of the paintbrush and reported the news:

Maurice Sendak might faint but a staff member of Caldwell Parish Library, knowing that the patrons of the community might object to the illustrations in *In the Night Kitchen*, solved the problem by diapering the little boy with white tempera paint. Other librarians might wish to do the same.[48]

When Ursula Nordstrom read her copy of *School Library Journal*, she erupted in anger. Since the book first arrived on the shelves, Sendak's editor had endured many complaints from parents about Mickey's nudity. One parent who wrote to Nordstrom reported that she burned her child's copy of the book. In her reply to the parent, Nordstrom defended Sendak, insisting that the author, through Mickey's story, is "able to speak to children directly."[49] Nordstrom added that of all the complaints she had received, none were from children. "I think young children will always react with delight to such a book as *In the Night Kitchen*, and that they will react creatively and wholesomely. It is only adults who feel threatened by Sendak's work."[50]

As it turned out, though, many school and public librarians elected to take the *School Library Journal's* advice and deface *In the Night Kitchen*. Indeed, efforts to censor *In the Night Kitchen* continued for years after the book was first published. Today, it is rare for librarians to physically alter the book, but efforts continue to ensure that it is not seen by children. Over the years, Sendak's publisher has heard complaints from parents in Michigan, Wisconsin, Texas, Illinois, and Minnesota, among other states. In Beloit, Wisconsin, for example, parents contended that the book is obscene and "desensitized children to nudity."[51]

In many cases, school board members and library officials have stood up to pressure and refused to alter the book or remove it from the shelves. In 1990, after parents in Morrisonville, New York, objected to the book and demanded it not be used in elementary school classrooms, the school board appointed a committee of teachers to assess the book's educational value. After hearing from the committee, the school board elected to retain it for classroom use. A similar ruling was rendered by the school board in Jacksonville, Florida, after a parent objected to the book.

Meanwhile, in Cornish, Maine, a parent filed a written complaint against use of *In the Night Kitchen* in elementary school classrooms, stating: "Child abuse. Children are taught their private parts are private. This book is contrary to teaching."[52] Again, after the school board assessed the complaint, *In the Night Kitchen* was permitted to remain in the classroom. The school board in Cornish called the book "a masterpiece example of the timeless theme of childhood fantasy . . . The story is certain to entertain readers of all ages."[53]

Of course, at the bottom of most of the complaints is a suspicion that Sendak intended to do more than tell an innocent story of a little boy's adventure in the magical Night Kitchen. Some parents, librarians, and critics suggested that Sendak truly intended to display a sexual image in the book. Writing in the scholastic journal *Elementary English*, critic Shelton L. Root said, "It just may be that America's children have been waiting with bated breath for this opportunity to vicariously wallow nude in cake dough and skinny dip in milk . . . Somehow, I doubt it."[54] David C. Davis, another critic writing in *Elementary English*, described *In the Night Kitchen* as "questionable nourishment for the very young members of our society."[55]

For his part, Sendak was shocked by the reaction to his book. When he conceived the idea for *In the Night Kitchen*, and began making rough sketches for the book, he did not know that he would be the first storybook artist to portray

Despite the controversy that often follows Maurice Sendak's work, he has won many awards throughout his career as author and illustrator. Shown here, Sendak smiles as he signs autographs after being presented with a lifetime achievement award from Child Magazine, *February 2004.*

the nudity of a child. Therefore, he hardly regarded himself as a trailblazer and was surprised to learn that no illustrator had included similar images throughout more than a century of storybook art in America. He said:

Unbeknowst to me, there had never been a picture of a frontal nude child in an American children's book. The only way it could be seen in many schools was if the teacher drew clothes on the child. The controversy reduced the book to such a stupid level.[56]

BANNED BOOKS

Each year, hundreds of books face censorship fights. Typically, a teacher assigns the book to students or a librarian orders it for the school library's shelves. The book may focus on an issue that some parents or other members of the community find objectionable. They raise concerns with the school board, which may order the book removed from the classroom or library or impose rules that strictly limit its availability to students. Every fall, the American Library Association sponsors Banned Books Week to call attention to censorship.

The truth is that in a society which prides itself on the First Amendment right of free speech, more and more challenges are issued against books each year. According to the ALA, parents and others challenged 458 books found in school and public libraries in 2003. In 2004, the organization said, 547 challenges were issued.

Any formal, written complaint filed with a school or public library against a book is seen as a challenge. Judith F. Krug, director of the ALA's Office for Intellectual Freedom, suspects that there may be many more challenges than those reported to her office. In fact, Krug believes that for every challenge reported to the ALA, another four or five may remain unreported. ALA President Carol Brey-Casiano said, "Not every book is right for every person, but providing a wide range of reading choices is vital for learning, exploration and imagination. The abilities to read, speak, think and express ourselves freely are core American values."[57]

Annually, the ALA announces a list of the 10 most-challenged titles. In 2004, the list included John Steinbeck's book *Of Mice and Men*, which can be found in middle- and high-school English classes throughout the United States. Steinbeck's book made the list because of the author's use of offensive language. The 2004 list of most-challenged books also included *In the Night Kitchen*. Indeed, 34 years after it was first published, the story of Mickey's after-dark adventure was still prompting a significant number of complaints.

BLUE CURTAINS IN THE JUSTICE DEPARTMENT

Should Sendak have depicted Mickey in the nude? Child psychology experts and other social critics are divided on the issue. In her book *Inside Picture Books*, an analysis of children's storybook literature, author Ellen Handler Spitz pointed out that one of the reasons the reaction against *In the Night Kitchen* was so great was that librarians feared other illustrators would follow Sendak's lead and, soon, images of naked children would dominate young people's books. That has not happened. "Their act was certainly an overreaction," Spitz wrote of the librarians. "Sendak's work started no trend; child nudity is still a rare sight in picture books."[58] Still, Spitz wondered whether all children could accept Sendak's images of Mickey. She pointed out that not all children are the same—they accept cultural images in different contexts and parents would do well to be wary of how their children would react when they start turning the pages of Sendak's book. "*In the Night Kitchen* is indisputably a fascinating work, but it is clearly not the right bedtime story for all children," she said.[59]

In contrast, author Judith Levine defended Sendak's use

of nudity in the book. In her book, *Harmful to Minors*—an analysis of censorship laws in America—Levine suggested that the mission "to scrub the public space clean of sexuality "[60] has been launched by the ultraconservative political and religious movement in America, and that before the so-called "religious right" gained political power during the administration of President Ronald Reagan in the 1980s, displays of nudity—in art museums, literature and other places in the public domain—were routine and accepted. She wrote:

> Artists and civil libertarians have resisted, but what was once controversial has become commonsensical. By the 1990s, commercial media all posted "harmful to minors" warnings before programs containing sexual language or images, and—a practice unheard of even a decade before and still considered ludicrous in Europe—American public art spaces routinely post similar advisories that an exhibition might be "inappropriate" for children. Many such exhibits display nothing more than paintings or sculptures of nudes.[61]

Levine's point proved to be timely. In 2002, the same year her book was published, U.S. Attorney General John Ashcroft ordered a curtain installed in the Justice Department's Great Hall in Washington, D.C., to mask the partial nudity of two statues. The Great Hall is used by the agency to stage press conferences, speeches, awards programs, and similar ceremonial events. The two statues have stood in the Great Hall since the 1930s, and before Ashcroft was appointed to the post by President George W. Bush, no other attorney general seemed bothered by the art on display.

The 12-foot-high statues include "Spirit of Justice," which depicts a partially-nude woman, and "Majesty of Law," which features a partially-nude man. But Ashcroft, a leader

Did you know...

The American government and courts have long grap-
pled with the question of defining obscenity. The law
that is applied to answer that question is the First
Amendment to the U.S. Constitution, which guarantees
the right of free speech. But is the publication of
pornography or even the simple portrayal of nudity—as
it is found in Maurice Sendak's *In the Night Kitchen*—
protected under the First Amendment?

The answer is not clear. Over the years, the U.S.
Supreme Court has tried many times to define obscenity. In 1964, in his ruling in an obscenity case, Justice
Potter Stewart summed up the frustration of the task
when, after examining an example of pornographic literature, said he could not explain to anybody exactly
what he considered obscene, "but I know it when I see
it."

In 1973, the court set a precedent that is followed
today, ruling that a book or film could be regarded as
obscene if the "average person, applying contemporary
community standards" would find the item's content to
be "patently offensive" and lacking "serious literary,
artistic, political or scientific value."

Certainly, that ruling left a lot of room for interpre-
tation and, over the years, courts and government
agencies have struggled with applying the Supreme
Court's standard to books, films, and other media. The
Federal Communications Commission, for example, has
used that standard to fine foul-mouthed radio disk
jockeys. As for *In the Night Kitchen*, even Sendak's
harshest critics would concede the book has artistic
and literary value and, therefore, his drawings of the
plucky [and naked] hero could not possibly be
regarded as obscene.

of the religious right, ordered a blue curtain hung in front of the statues. When Ashcroft stepped down in 2004, his successor, Attorney General Alberto Gonzales, quietly ordered the curtain removed.

According to Levine, a basic principle preached by the ultraconservative religious movement in America is that parents have the responsibility to tell their children about sex and explain what body parts are for. She suggested, though, that parents routinely avoid the issue. They may be too embarrassed to have that talk with their children, or simply too busy, or they may believe that their children already know all there is to know. And so, she said, children are forced to figure it out on their own. Wouldn't it be more fulfilling for children, she asked, if they are exposed to public art—and storybooks—where the issue is raised in a tasteful and intelligent manner? She wrote:

> Children absorb from their families attitudes toward love, the body, authority, and equality; they are trained in tolerance and kindness or their opposite at home. A few live in families comfortable enough to discuss the nitty-gritty details of sex. But the vast majority learn these from the wider world.[62]

CENSORSHIP BY MUTILATION

Sendak has never publicly explained what prompted him to send Mickey through the Night Kitchen in the nude, other than to suggest that the book tells the story of a dream and people who have criticized the story have evidently never dreamed of themselves in the nude. But he has lashed out at the librarians who have defaced the book or removed it from their shelves as well as parents and others who have burned or otherwise destroyed *In the Night Kitchen* to keep it away from the eyes of children. Defacing the images of Mickey, he wrote, "reduced a book I had worked on for more than three years to nothing more than sheer idiocy."[63]

He also insists that young children are a lot more comfortable with their own nudity than adults may think, and they do not learn that the image of a naked body is inappropriate until an adult tells them. Sendak complained that covering up images of nudity in public art in America is simply a reaction by adults who feel the image of a nude body is pornographic. "We prefer the blur; the fig leaf, the diaper," he said.[64]

Back in 1972, when Nordstrom read the item in the *School Library Journal* about the Caldwell Parish librarian's hand-painted diaper, she asked librarians to sign a petition denouncing the censorship of *In the Night Kitchen*. More than 400 librarians signed the petition, many of whom sent Nordstrom personal notes in support of Sendak and the efforts of the publisher to keep the book on the shelves and unaltered. Nordstrom wrote:

> At first the thought of librarians painting diapers or pants on the naked hero of Sendak's book might seem amusing, merely a harmless eccentricity on the part of some prim few. On reconsideration, however, this behavior should be recognized for what it is: an act of censorship by mutilation rather than by obvious suppression.
>
> A private individual who owns a book is free, of course, to do with it as he pleases; he may destroy his property, or cherish it, even paint clothes on any naked figures that appear in it. But it is an altogether different matter when a librarian disfigures a book purchased with public funds—thereby editing the work of the author—and then presents this distortion to the library's patrons.
>
> The mutilation of Sendak's *In the Night Kitchen* by certain librarians must not be allowed to have an intimidating effect

on creators and publishers of books for children. We, as writers, illustrators, publishers, critics, and librarians, deeply concerned with preserving the First Amendment freedoms for everyone involved in the process of communicating ideas, vigorously protest this exercise of censorship.[65]

Those were strong words, to be sure, but as history shows, challenges to Sendak's book and efforts to censor Mickey's nudity continue. According to Sendak, sympathetic librarians regularly smuggle defaced copies of *In the Night Kitchen* out of their libraries and mail the copies to him to show that the censorship of his work persists. Sendak said of Nordstrom's petition:

> I wish I could report that it all made a difference. It did not. The small but steady stream of expurgated copies that find their way to my house testify to that sad fact. The heat is still on Mickey.[66]

In 1991, Sendak was asked to design a poster for the American Library Association's annual convention. He quickly agreed, and adopted some scenes from *In the Night Kitchen* for the poster. The poster features Mickey flying his bread dough airplane over the Night Kitchen "city" while beneath the airplane a second image of Mickey appears, reading a book and floating, naked, in a bottle of milk.

The person who has had the most influence on Maurice Sendak's work is William Blake, pictured here. This 18th- and early 19th-century English poet illustrated his own verse with colorful images of mystical creatures. Blake's influence is most easily seen in Where the Wild Things Are—*the wild things are similar to Blake's "Tyger"—and* Outside Over There, *in which Ida loses her sense of innocence in order to rescue her sibling.*

5

The Art of
Storytelling

ALTHOUGH HE DREW PICTURES for storybooks long before he started writing his own words, when Maurice Sendak develops an idea for a book he always envisions the story first. Later, he roughs out the images. By being both writer and illustrator, Sendak has learned that the words and pictures must complement each other—the words must provide the beginning of the message the author is trying to convey and the pictures must then complete the story. He said:

> You must never illustrate exactly what is written. You must find a
> space in the text so that pictures can do the work. Then you must

let words take over where words do it best. It's a funny kind of juggling act, which takes a lot of technique and experience to keep the rhythm going.

You have worked out the text so supple, that it stops and goes, stops and goes, with pictures shrewdly interspersed. The pictures, too, become so supple that there's an interchangeability between them and the words; they each tell two stories at the same time. The peculiar gift in being an illustrator is that one has an odd affinity for words—it's natural to interpret them, like a composer who thinks music while reading poetry. The illustrator's first job is to comprehend deeply the nature of his text, then to give life to that comprehension in his own medium, the picture. I like to think of myself as setting words to pictures. A true picture book is a visual poem.[67]

THE INFLUENCE OF WILLIAM BLAKE

Illustrators and writers owe a debt to others in their fields who have come before them. Although many talented writers have set their own standard and developed writing styles and techniques that are uniquely their own, there is no question that they have all been influenced by other writers—authors whom they read as children or young adults from whose writing they learned about the craft of storytelling. Illustrators are similarly influenced by others whose works have impacted the way they render their own images for a story.

Sendak said the artist and writer who has had the most influence on his work is William Blake, the 18th- and early 19th-century English poet who illustrated his own verse with colorful images of mystical creatures. Blake was obsessed with the notion of young children waking from their innocence to discover a cruel, adult-oriented world. Two of his most familiar poems are "The Lamb" and "The Tyger."

Sendak said, "Blake is unquestionably important, my cornerstone in many ways. Nobody before him ever told me that childhood was such a damned serious business."[68]

Certainly, Sendak's readers can find the influence of Blake in many of his storybooks. In *Where the Wild Things Are*, Max discovers fierce beasts—Blake's "tygers"—awaiting him at the end of a long journey, which could very well be his childhood. At the beginning of *Outside Over There*, Ida is an innocent child whose naiveté [she is fooled when an ice sculpture is substituted for her baby sister] causes her to lose her sister to goblins. Only by venturing "over there"—by growing up—is she able to retrieve the baby. And in the story of *In the Night Kitchen*, Mickey actually does wake up from an innocent sleep to find mischief going on in the kitchen below. He must use his guile to escape from the bumbling bakers.

INSPIRATION OFTEN PERSONAL

Of course, Blake is only one source of influence for Sendak. Like all authors and artists, Sendak draws his inspirations from other people, places, and life experiences. He may be riding in a car one day and see a homeless boy's feet sticking out of a box and conceive the idea for a story about homeless children, as he did with *We Are All in the Dumps With Jack and Guy*. Or, he may recall the little girl named Rosie from his old Brooklyn neighborhood who enjoyed playacting for her friends, which led to *The Sign on Rosie's Door*. For *In the Night Kitchen*, Sendak was inspired to draw his three bakers to resemble the movie comic Oliver Hardy after seeing one of Hardy's movies, *Nothing but Trouble*, on television as he started work on the book. Sometimes, the inspiration can be very personal. In 1966, Sendak wrote and illustrated *Higglety Pigglety Pop! or There Must be More to*

Did you know...

Maurice Sendak wrote and illustrated his book *Higglety Pigglety Pop! or There Must be More to Life* as a tribute to his terrier Jennie. The dog had lived with Sendak for 14 years before her death in 1967. "She was a baby, child, companion, and best friend," Sendak said in the 1991 biography *Maurice Sendak* by Amy Sonheim. In fact, over the years Sendak inserted illustrations of Jennie in many of his books, including *Kenny's Window*, as well as stories he illustrated for other authors such as Sesyle Joslin's *What Do You Say, Dear?*

In 1967, Sendak left Jennie in the care of a friend and traveled to England. While being interviewed on a British television show, Sendak suddenly felt ill. Indeed, he was not able to finish the interview. At the age of 38, Sendak had suffered a heart attack. "I was amazed," he said. "I couldn't believe it was happening—that my mission could be cut short like that."

Sendak moved into a convalescent home in England to recover, but soon learned that his dog Jennie was ill. Against the advice of his doctor, Sendak checked himself out and returned to the United States where he was reunited with his dog. A short time later, Jennie died.

Sadly, his own illness and the death of his dog were not the only troubles Sendak had to overcome. While recovering from his heart attack he learned that his mother, Sadie, was ill with cancer. To endure the grief caused by the loss of his dog and his mother's illness, Sendak worked hard on *Higglety Pigglety Pop! or There Must be More to Life*. The book was published in July 1968, just a month after his mother's death.

Life as a tribute to his terrier Jennie, who had just died. Sendak said:

> None of my books come about through "ideas," or by thinking of a particular subject and exclaiming, "Gee, that's terrific; I'll just put it down!" They never happen quite that way. They well up. Just as dreams come to us at night, feelings come to me, and I rush to put them down. But these fantasies have to be given a physical form, so I build a kind of house around them—the story—and the painting of the house is the picture-making. Essentially, however, it's a dream or fantasy.[69]

Higglety Pigglety Pop! or There Must be More to Life is the story of a dog who has everything—"a round pillow upstairs and a square pillow downstairs"[70]—but thinks there is more to life than the luxuries she enjoys at home. So Jennie ventures into the world outside, where she finds a job as a nanny to a bratty baby. When Jennie saves the baby from a lion, she is awarded the leading role in the "World Mother Goose Theater." Sixty-nine pages in length, *Higglety Pigglety Pop! or There Must be More to Life* is Sendak's longest book.

Sendak tells the story in short, declarative sentences. Certainly, there is magic in the story: the dog speaks English, a cat drives a milk cart, and the bratty baby grows up in an instant, but the book does not include the mystical journeys of Sendak's storybooks—no long trip across the ocean, no flight by Ida in search of her sister, no trip by Mickey to the Milky Way. Indeed, Sendak said *Higglety Pigglety Pop! or There Must be More to Life* is a clear example of storytelling in which the words tell some of the story, then make way for the pictures to do the rest. Sendak said:

> I wanted the writing to be as terse and as tough as Jennie was, almost acidic—to contain nothing sentimental or romantic.

But because I brought so much sentiment to the story I wanted the pictures to be as romantic as the text was terse. And they are. The illustrations are doing what the text is not doing; it's a matter of reading between the lines.[71]

MONTHS OF REVISING

According to Sendak, even the simplest stories that may span no more than a few hundred words often take years to write. Sometimes, he will rework the text dozens or even hundreds of times before he is satisfied with the way it reads. For example, in the finished story of *Where the Wild Things Are*, Sendak brought the tale to a close as Max realizes he misses his home. In one of the earlier versions of the story, when Max announces his intentions to leave his new friends, the wild things voice their protests.

> But Max didn't care because the Wild Things
> never loved him best of all—or let
> him eat from grown-up plates
>
> or showed him how to call long distance.
> So Max gave up being King of Where the Wild Things Are.
>
> "Wild Things Are Child Things,"
> said Max as he steered his boat
> back over the year and in and
> out of weeks and through the day.[72]

After looking over the prose, Sendak concluded that the words would dominate the action on the pages. Essentially, he found, there were too many words for the reader, describing too much. With all that written description, Sendak wondered what else the pictures would be able to show. The text also provided Max with a bit of smugness that Sendak did not want to see in the character at that point in the story. In the final version, Sendak eliminated the smugness and shortened the prose, leaving himself room to provide very descriptive drawings. His final version read simply:

"Now stop!" Max said and sent the wild things off to bed without supper. And Max the king of all wild things was lonely and wanted to be where someone loved him best of all.[73]

As for the drawings that Sendak eventually provided, the pages in which those words are featured show a melancholy Max, sitting on a stool at the entrance of his grand tent, while the wild things doze in the woods nearby. Clearly, the illustration tells a lot that Sendak could not possibly fit into a dozen or so words on the page. Sendak said:

With me, everything begins with writing. No pictures at all—you just shut the Polaroid off; you don't want to be seduced by pictures because then you begin to write for pictures. Images come in language, language, language: in phrases, in verbal constructs, in poetry, whatever. I've never spent less than two years on the text of one of my picture books, even though each of them is approximately 380 words long. Only when the text is finished—when my editor thinks it's finished—do I begin the pictures. *Then* I put the film in my head.[74]

STIRRING A MYSTERIOUS SOUP

Once Sendak is satisfied with the story, he will draw the pictures. For Sendak, providing the illustrations for one of his books or for a story written by another author can range from being a relatively simple task to a very lengthy and complicated undertaking. Usually, he starts with simple sketches using a pencil or pen and ink. These sketches are not much more than doodles. In the book, *Wings of an Artist*, he explained:

> I have been doodling with ink and watercolor on paper all my life. It's my way of stirring up my imagination to see what I can find hidden in my head. I call the results dream pictures, fantasy sketches, and even brain-sharpening exercises. They are the only homework I've ever energetically applied myself to, the only school that ever taught me anything . . . Spontaneous sketching gives me great pleasure. I recommend doodling as an excellent exercise in stirring up the unconscious, just as you would stir up some mysterious soup all the while hoping it tastes good.[75]

For each book, a major hurdle Sendak must overcome is what sort of backdrop he wants to use to frame the pictures. For example, in *In the Night Kitchen* he wanted to give Mickey a sort of New York adventure, so he designed a 1930s-style cityscape composed of cereal boxes, ketchup bottles and other features Mickey would find in a kitchen. *We Are All in the Dumps With Jack and Guy* was meant to be a contemporary story about homelessness so Sendak illustrated, essentially, a modern city trash dump.

Sometimes, the job calls for more than just drawing familiar scenes from everyday life. In 1973, Sendak was called on to illustrate a two-volume work of stories by Jacob and Wilhelm Grimm titled *The Juniper Tree and Other Tales from Grimm*. The brothers Grimm were 19th-century German scholars whose study of old European folklore led them to collect and publish volumes of fairy tales. Sendak wanted to give the book an authentic flavor of the era, so before starting the drawings he traveled to Germany where he visited an

In 1973, Maurice Sendak illustrated a two-volume work of stories by Jacob and Wilhelm Grimm titled The Juniper Tree and Other Tales from Grimm. *The brothers Grimm, pictured here, were 19th-century German scholars whose study of old European folklore led them to collect and publish volumes of fairy tales. Sendak traveled to Germany in order to give the book an authentic flavor of the era.*

old castle and toured German forests and many small villages where he studied the medieval architecture. He hoped that his first-hand look at old Europe would give his illustrations something more than "just an American, 1970s point of view."[76] Indeed, for *The Juniper Tree and Other Tales from Grimm*, Sendak rendered somber black and white drawings that appeared as though they had been drawn in medieval times.

For *Outside Over There*, Sendak wished to give the story a similar old-world backdrop, suggesting that Ida's adventure takes place in 18th-century Europe. This time, instead of traveling to Europe for first-hand research, Sendak spent many months studying the clothing styles of the era, then hired a photographer and two children to work as models. The children included a 9-year-old girl named Esme who portrayed Ida, and a 14-month-old baby named Natalie who took the role of Ida's sister. To pick the children for the roles, Sendak had the photographer make a number of test shots on instant Polaroid film, then the artist and photographer sifted through the candidates until Sendak found the two models who most closely resembled the characters he intended to draw.

He had the children dress in costumes, then posed them in scenes he wished to duplicate in the book. He instructed the photographer to take many pictures of the two children, then Sendak composed drawings from the photographic images. He said:

> These are realistic touches that just can't be fudged, and I wanted to get them absolutely right. The pictures have a super-real stopped-in-time quality. They're better than I had any right to hope for.[77]

THE NITTY-GRITTY CREATIVE PROCESS

As with the text, illustrations go through many revisions as well. For *In the Night Kitchen*, Sendak first experimented with drawing the bakers as animals—a dog, cat, and pig. Also, in early versions of the book he did not draw the dreamy New York City skyline—his simple sketches of the hero only showed Mickey acting out the adventure Sendak had written. The sketches showed Mickey climbing up a milk bottle, falling in, then escaping, and so on. Sendak recalled:

> There were serious problems. I had to get Mickey from the bed, down to the kitchen, up to the sky, into the milk bottle, down from the milk bottle, and back into his bed. It was just a lumbering, difficult job getting that kid to budge.[78]

Sketching Mickey's journey was an important step in the process, because it showed Sendak whether the pictures would do what he wanted them to do in the end—take over for the text and help tell the story.

The next step in Sendak's illustrating process is to prepare what is known as a "dummy"—basically, a rough sketch of the whole book, showing the illustrations that will appear on each page. In the dummy, each individual picture is known as a "study" drawing. Producing the dummy gives the illustrator a chance to see the whole story as it unfolds on paper. Then, if something is wrong—if the pictures are not flowing properly or carrying the text the way Sendak wants them to, he can pull pictures out of the dummy and redraw them. Sendak said:

> This becomes the unconscious shaping of the book. What's interesting is that I always do the initial dummy fairly quickly, and then I go into the study drawings where I correct if some-

thing is wrong with my layout. But I hardly ever have to correct the overall scheme. Which means that the first instinctual thing is right.[79]

When the dummy meets his expectations, Sendak will provide final versions of the drawings—adding color if he has decided to produce the book in color.

Sometimes the drawings fail even though Sendak has done the most meticulous planning before rendering them onto paper. For example, Sendak first started planning *Where the Wild Things Are* in 1955—eight years before it was published. Originally, he planned to title the book *Where the Wild Horses Are*, and tell the story of a young boy following clues to a place where he finds wild horses. The story read:

> Once a boy asked where the wild horses are.
> Nobody could tell him.
> So he asked himself where the wild horses are.
> And he answered, they must be this way.
> Luckily the way led through his own room.
> He found signs pointing in the right direction. [80]

Of course, the final version turned out to be a much different story. Nevertheless, when Sendak believed he had worked out the story and sat down at his drawing board and prepared to sketch his ideas for the illustrations, he discovered one troubling fact about his artistic ability: he was incapable of drawing a horse.

Sendak thought hard for inspiration and finally decided to substitute monsters for horses. But what type of monster should he draw? To solve his dilemma, Sendak drew on thoughts of his childhood—how he hated the occasions when aunts and uncles came over for dinner on Sundays. He hated when they joined the family for dinner and pinched his cheeks, telling him, "You're so cute I could eat you up."[81] He found his relatives to be quite obnoxious—to be, well, monsters. Indeed, their constant and gruesome promise to *eat him up* remained with Sendak for many years and, in the final version of the book, Sendak makes Max truly monstrous when he has the boy threaten to eat his mother. He said:

> Originally, I didn't want them to be wild "things"; I wanted them to be wild horses. In fact, the original title was *Where the Wild Horses Are*. The dilemma arose when it became obvious that I couldn't draw horses. So I had to think of something I *could* draw. Because the truth about the creative process is that it's a hard-line, nitty-gritty business of what you can and cannot do—what your limitations are as an artist. I tried to use monsters from the antique world—griffins and other such creatures. But they weren't satisfactory because they didn't come out of me; they were borrowed monsters.
>
> Then, very gradually, these other creatures began to appear on my drawing paper, and I knew right away they were my relatives. They were my uncles and aunts. It wasn't that they were monstrous people; it was simply that I didn't care for them when I was a child because they were rude, and because they ruined every Sunday . . . They pinched us and poked us and said those tedious, boring things that grown-ups say, and my sister and my brother and I sat there in total dismay and rage. The only fun we had was later, giggling over their grotesque faces—the huge noses, the spiraling hair pouring out of the wrong places.[82]

Maurice Sendak listens to a variety of classical music while he works, but he most enjoys music written by Wolfgang Amadeus Mozart. The 18th-century Austrian composer, shown here, is one of the most important figures in the history of music having written over 600 pieces of music. He was also a Freemason, and many say that his opera for children, The Magic Flute, *has Masonic themes and symbols written into it. When Sendak designed the sets and costumes for* The Magic Flute, *he, too, drew inspiration from the symbols of Freemasonry.*

6

Sendak on Stage

WHEN MAURICE SENDAK SITS DOWN at his drawing table, he insists on working to the sounds of classical music. Sendak enjoys the symphonies, sonatas, fugues, and operas of many composers, to be sure, but in Sendak's mind the work of Wolfgang Amadeus Mozart stands above all others. "To me, the best of all art form is music," Sendak said, "and perhaps opera is my favorite, and the best, best, best of all that is Mozart."[83] In his books, Sendak has paid tribute to Mozart. For example, on one of the final pages of *Outside Over There*, the young heroine Ida carries her baby sister home past a distant image of Mozart composing the opera *The Magic Flute*.

The 18th-century Austrian composer is regarded as one of the most important figures in the history of music. A genius who mastered the piano, organ and violin as a young child, by the age of 6 years old Mozart was already composing music. At 14, he composed his first opera. By the time he died—of typhoid fever at the age of 35—Mozart had written more than 600 pieces of music, including such well-known operas as *The Marriage of Figaro, Don Giovanni*, and *The Magic Flute*, his opera for children.

The Magic Flute, which was first performed in 1791, is the story of the adventures of Tamino, who pursues his young bride Pamina through the realm of the mysterious yet benevolent Sarastro with the help of a magical flute, which can tame fierce beasts that threaten his journey. Among the characters in the opera are the comical Papageno; Pamina's mother, the evil Queen of the Night; three genies who assist Tamino's search for his beloved; and a brutal henchman named Monostatos. Sendak said:

> I think some of the most touching moments in *The Magic Flute* have to do with children. Much of the opera focuses on the confusion of an adolescent girl. Is her mother crazy? Is the man she loves crazy? Has the solemn Sarastro saved her or kidnapped her? Isn't this very much what life is like for young people?[84]

Many of Sendak's books have included musical themes. In *Higglety Pigglety Pop! or There Must be More to Life*, Jennie is rewarded at the end of the book with the starring role in a musical play, and in *The Sign on Rosie's Door* the main character enjoys playacting and singing for her friends. In 1975, a theatrical company in Brussels, Belgium, proposed that Sendak adapt *Where the Wild Things Are* to opera. Sendak provided the "libretto," which is the story, and also designed the sets and costumes. Meanwhile, the British composer and conductor Oliver Knussen wrote the music. After working on the project for nearly three years, Sendak received an offer from the Houston Grand Opera in the United States: would he design the costumes and sets for the opera company's production of *The Magic Flute*?

Actually, when Sendak received the offer from the Houston Grand Opera he found himself with as much work as he thought he could handle. In addition to wrapping up his work on the operatic version of *Where the Wild Things Are*, he was collaborating with the American songwriter Carole King on developing an animated version of *The Sign on Rosie's Door*, which would be televised in 1975 on the CBS network as *Really Rosie*. Later, Sendak and King adapted *Really Rosie* as a stage version, which debuted in New York's Chelsea Theater Center in 1980. Meanwhile, he was hard at work on a storybook, *In Grandpa's House*. And so, while juggling all those projects, Sendak had to decide whether he wanted to take on the additional burden of designing the sets and costumes for a production of one of his favorite operas written by his favorite composer. Needless to say, he quickly agreed. He said, "Since I was sixteen, Mozart had been my savior and *The Magic Flute* was my life preserver."[85]

INSPIRED BY FREEMASONRY

Both Mozart and Emanuel Schikaneder, the man who wrote the libretto for *The Magic Flute*, were Freemasons. Formally known as the Grand Lodge of Free and Accepted Masons, Freemasonry grew out of trade guilds formed by English stone-cutters. The movement spread throughout the rest of Europe and eventually to America. Freemasonry drew many important intellectuals, writers, educators, and business leaders to its ranks; among its members in America were Benjamin Franklin and George Washington.

Freemasons believe in civic-mindedness, religious toler-
ance, and democratic values—ideas that would form the
foundations of American society. But in Europe, during
Mozart's day, those ideas were still regarded as radical
notions. Freemasons have performed many charitable
endeavors over the years, but for a time the society insisted
on conducting its meetings in secret, raising the suspicions
of outsiders who believed the Freemasons were hatching
evil schemes. Indeed, members of the monarchy as well as
leaders of the Roman Catholic Church—a very influential
institution in Austria—were suspicious of the Freemasons'
motives.

Some historians believe Mozart and Schikaneder placed
many Masonic themes and symbols into *The Magic Flute*.
To start, they set the opera in ancient Egypt; over the years,
the Freemasons have adopted many symbols from the Middle East—the swords known as scimitars as well as pyramids, for example—as emblems of their society. Further, it
is suggested that the character of the Queen of the Night represents the Austrian Queen Maria Theresa, who opposed
Freemasonry, while other characters in the opera represent
political leaders who were significant figures in 18th-cen-
tury Austrian Freemasonry.

To design the sets and costumes, Sendak drew inspiration
from the symbols of Freemasonry. To decorate the opera's
scenes, he used stone columns and arches, statues of brood-
ing and bearded Egyptian-style gods, rocky steps leading up
to pyramids and airy temples surrounded by palm fronds.
For the costumes, Sendak based his designs on a mixture of
old and contemporary Masonic styles. While some characters wear robes and gowns that suggest ancient Egyptian
dress, others wear accessories from 21st-century meetings
at Masonic lodges in America, such as the sequined and

tasseled conical hat known as the fez. Playwright Tony Kushner, who has collaborated with Sendak on several projects, said, "Sendak's design is, it seems to me, absolutely consonant with Mozart's and librettist Emanuel Schikaneder's response to the secret order, or at least what we may infer their response to have been."[86]

During the next few years, Sendak provided designs for many other musical productions, including another opera by Mozart, *Idomeneo*, and operas *The Love for Three Oranges* by Sergey Prokofiev and *The Cunning Little Vixen* by Leos Janacek. He worked again with Knussen to adapt *Higglety Pigglety Pop! or There Must be More to Life* into an operatic version, performed by the Glyndebourne Opera in England. For that production, he also wrote the libretto.

THE NUTCRACKER

In 1981, while Sendak was finishing his work on *The Love for Three Oranges*, he was asked by the Pacific Northwest Ballet in Seattle, Washington, to design the costumes and sets for the company's production of *The Nutcracker*. Presented at Christmastime each year by many ballet companies, *The Nutcracker* is one of the most familiar ballet productions featured on stages in the United States and elsewhere. It is the musical version of a children's story written in 1816 by German author E.T.A. Hoffmann. In 1891 and 1892, the Russian composer Pyotr Ilyich Tchaikovsky composed the music that would be set to the story in the ballet.

The Nutcracker tells of the adventure of a young girl named Clara who, on Christmas Eve, is given a magical toy nutcracker by a mysterious dinner guest named Herr Drosselmeier. During the night, Clara wakes to discover that the Nutcracker has come alive in order to lead her brother's toy soldiers in a battle against the Mouse King.

The Nutcracker *is one of the most popular ballet productions featured on stages in the United States. In 1981, the Pacific Northwest Ballet in Seattle, Washington, asked Maurice Sendak to design costumes and sets for their production, shown above. Written in 1816 by E.T.A. Hoffmann, Pyotr Ilyich Tchaikovsky composed music to adapt the story into a ballet. Sendak helped rewrite the story for the Pacific North-west Ballet, adding elements not found in most other productions of* The Nutcracker.

Sendak was wary of participating in the project. He felt *The Nutcracker* had been performed so often that he could not bring a fresh approach to the story. Even more importantly, he had never designed sets and costumes for a ballet and was unsure whether his ideas could translate to a stage that must be kept largely open for the wide-ranging movements of the dancers. After meeting with Kent Stowell, the artistic director for the ballet company, Sendak developed an enthusiasm for the project and soon immersed himself in the story. Indeed, he became more than just a costume and set designer. For the Pacific Northwest Ballet's production, Sendak helped rewrite the story, adding elements not found in most other productions of *The Nutcracker*. He said:

> Most of my doubts and worries were put to rest when Kent and I met for the first time early in 1981 in New York City. I liked him immediately for not wanting me to do *The Nutcracker* for all the obvious reasons but rather because he wished me to join him in a leap into the unknown. He suggested we abandon the predictable *Nutcracker* and find a fresh version that did honor to Hoffmann, Tchaikovsky, and ourselves.[87]

Sendak and Stowell wanted to make their version of *The Nutcracker* closer to Hoffmann's. Over the years, various ballet productions had translated the story to fit the talents of their dancers or the interpretations of their choreographers and musical directors. Sendak believed that with these changes Hoffmann's original story had suffered. To begin with, Sendak found that the role of Clara had been condensed, making her less important to the story, which invariably concentrated on the character of the Nutcracker. In many prior productions, after Clara is given the Nutcracker and wakes to find he has come alive, she hardly participates in the rest of the ballet. Sendak decided to change that, and the first thing he did was to make Clara older. (In previously produced versions, she is portrayed as a 7-year-old child, but in the Pacific Northwest Ballet version she would be 12.)

JUMPING OUT OF HIS STORYBOOKS

Sendak turned *The Nutcracker* into a coming-of-age story, showing how Clara has reached the threshold of womanhood with a wide-eyed wonderment of all things around her.

Did you know...

In 1999, Maurice Sendak provided the illustrations for a story that shows just how much fun ballet can be. The story, titled *Swine Lake*, was written by Sendak's friend James Marshall, who died in 1992. Before Marshall died, he wrote an unpublished story about a wolf who attends a ballet performed by pigs with the sole idea of dining on the dancers, but soon becomes so enthralled by the production that he joins the pigs on stage.

After his experience working on a very complicated ballet production for *The Nutcracker* and a much simpler ballet staging for *Where the Wild Things Are*, Sendak found he was able to tell the story of ballet in a humorous context.

"The story was perfect," Sendak said of *Swine Lake* in an interview with the magazine *BookPage*. "I've done a big ballet and a small ballet and I know how to make professionally fun of it. I know where it's silly, and I know where it's wonderful. And all of Jim's ballet scenes were deliriously funny."

Sendak has a lot of fun with the story, sprinkling a liberal dose of puns throughout his illustrations. For example, in the book he calls the production company the "Boarshoi Ballet," making a joke out of the name of the renowned Russian ballet troupe, the Bolshoi Ballet. Sendak names the theater the "New 'Hamsterdam' Theater." The local newspaper is titled *The Daily Bacon*. And the name of the production, *Swine Lake*, is a joke made out of the name of composer Pyotr Ilyich Tchaikovsky's most famous ballet, *Swan Lake*.

He made many other changes while preserving the integrity of the ballet and, of course, the music by Tchaikovsky. For example, he made the story darker, and the character of Herr Drosselmeier, the wizard who brings the toys to life, much more mysterious. Like his books, Sendak blurs the line in *The Nutcracker* between fantasy and reality. He also added a scene known as "The Story of the Hard Nut" in which the baby Princess Pirlipat is bitten by the mother of the Mouse King, transforming the child into a hideous beast. In retribution, the Mouse King's mother is killed by a handsome prince who turns out to be an ancestor of Herr Drosselmeier. To take revenge, the Mouse King imprisons the prince in the body of the toy nutcracker.

Sendak wanted to restore that scene to the ballet because he thought it would help develop the relationship between Clara and Herr Drosselmeier and set the stage for the epic battle between the toy soldiers and the mice. Sendak wrote the scene, which in the Pacific Northwest production spanned a mere three minutes. The problem with including the scene, though, is that there was no music for it. That issue was resolved when he recalled a piece of music played in Tchaikovsky's opera *The Queen of Spades*. In that opera, Tchaikovsky employed and adapted a brief series of notes written by Mozart. The music seemed perfect for *The Nutcracker*, and was soon adapted to the Pacific Northwest's production. "Tchaikovsky adored Mozart and wrote a number of compositions in homage to this master and my particular hero," Sendak said. "So there he was, smack in the middle of this production, the great papa, so to speak, of all involved."[88]

For the set and costume designs, Sendak stayed true to the European backdrop of the story, but he made certain to endow the sets with cartoonish images that often jump out of his storybooks. For example, Sendak designed a towering image of Herr Drosselmeier that grows out of a grandfather clock. For the Mouse King, Sendak designed a 27-foot puppet that included 17 moving pieces. The Christmas tree designed specifically for the production weighed half a ton and featured 1,000 light bulbs. (During the ballet, the tree grows on stage to a height of 28 feet.) It took nearly 40 stage hands to maneuver the Mouse King, the Christmas tree, and the other props Sendak designed for the ballet. Kushner said:

> My favorite of Sendak's *Nutcracker* drawings is his show curtain, on which that Christmas cliché, the Nutcracker's face is spread; Sendak has . . . projected that over-familiar [face] into a gasp-inducing, spine-tingling mask of madness, dental aggression, astonishment or anguished dread, surprised recognition: this, Sendak is telling us, is what we identify as the trademark face of Christmas.[89]

For months prior to the premiere, Sendak found himself repeatedly traveling from his home in Connecticut to Seattle to work on the designs and help guide the ballet into production. With so many technical details and problems to overcome, he worried that *The Nutcracker* would fall short of his expectations. Shortly before the ballet's premiere, Sendak wrote in his journal:

> Disaster strikes: floor is the wrong color, no one can dance, tree is sticking, bits of set get torn, fall down, raw anxiety . . . Totally depressed. I feel the set is a huge fatally flawed bit of junk, it is my failure."[90]

The Nutcracker premiered on December 13, 1983. It proved to be enormously successful and has remained a staple in the Pacific Northwest Ballet's repertoire. Each winter, some 100,000 people attend the ballet's performance in

Seattle. In 1986, a movie version was filmed. Sendak has also produced a storybook version of *The Nutcracker*. On the night the ballet opened in Seattle, Sendak wrote in his journal, "Opening night. Audience yells head off, a great success despite many technical flaws."[91]

Following the production of *The Nutcracker*, Sendak went on to design the sets and costumes for even more musical productions. After the adaptation of *Where the Wild Things Are* into an opera, Sendak worked with composer Randall Woolf to create a ballet version of the story for the American Repertory Ballet of Princeton, New Jersey. It premiered in 1997. Later, the ballet version of *Where the Wild Things Are* toured the United States.

Sendak discovered another musical work for which he used his talents to bring to the stage. The opera, titled *Brundibar*, contains many elements of magic and fantasy. Unlike *The Nutcracker* and *The Magic Flute*, which are light-hearted and often comical children's fantasies, *Brundibar* is a much more sinister story, retelling one of the darkest chapters in the history of mankind—the murders of millions of people during World War II.

In 2003, Maurice Sendak discovered Brundibar, originally written as an opera in 1938 by Hans Krasa. He wanted to produce a storybook version of Brundibar and enlisted his friend and playwright Tony Kushner to write both an English language version of the opera as well as the story for the book. Kushner, pictured here, is the Pulitzer Prize-winning author of "Angels in America."

7

Sendak's Holocaust Stories

AS A TEENAGER, MAURICE SENDAK learned the horrific truth about what happened to members of his family who were left behind in Poland during World War II: many of them died in Nazi concentration camps. The Nazi plan to exterminate the Jews and other "undesirables" of Europe—gypsies, communists, homosexuals, intellectuals, and political agitators, among others—has been labeled by historians as the "Holocaust." Some six million Jews as well as millions of others were murdered by the Nazis during the war years, most of them put to death in gas ovens.

The horrors of the Holocaust have never been far from Sendak's thoughts. After his parents arrived in America and married, they worked very hard to save money so they could buy steamship passages for their aunts, uncles, cousins, and other family members who were still living in Poland. But they ran out of time and were unable to save everyone. In an National Public Radio interview, Sendak related:

> All their first income was spent on bringing one aunt, then an uncle, then another uncle, then another aunt, then my grand-mother, till finally all but one brother on [my mother's] side were all here. Then they were going to turn to my father's side, but it was too late. That was in the thirties. There was no getting Jews out of Europe at that point. Growing up during the war was tough, having to live through that in all its com-plexity. It colors your life forever.[92]

Critics believe Sendak has woven Holocaust themes into many of his books. An example often given is the fact that Mickey faces death in an oven in the story *In the Night Kitchen*. Far more apparent, though, are Sendak's illustra-tions for a Wilhelm Grimm story titled *Dear Mili: An Old Tale*, which was published as a storybook in 1988. The story, written by Grimm in 1816, tells of a mother who sends her daughter into a forest to escape a war. The girl is led by her guardian angel to the home of Saint Joseph, where she lives for three days. When Mili leaves the house, St. Joseph gives her a rosebud and she discovers that the three days she spent in the house has really been 30 years. At the conclusion of the story, Mili is reunited with a very old woman who turns out to be her mother, but both die in their sleep as the rose-bud blooms into a flower. Sendak gave the story a definite Holocaust message, rendering images of concentration camps, prisoners of war and Jewish gravesites in the pages of the storybook and basing the character of Mili on Anne Frank, the Dutch teenager whose diary tells the gripping story of her family's ordeal hiding from the Nazis in an attic in Amsterdam.

As part of the story, Sendak has included an image of Mozart leading a choir of young singers. According to Sendak, the children are from the French village Izieu who were murdered by the notorious Nazi Klaus Barbie near the end of World War II. Following the war, Barbie successfully evaded justice but in 1983 he was found living in Bolivia. He was deported to France, where he was tried, convicted, and sentenced to life imprisonment. Barbie died in prison in 1991. Sendak said:

> I became absorbed with the fate of those children during Barbie's trial . . . and when I illustrated *Dear Mili* I took some of them and put them in paradise with Mozart, who is my favorite creature in the whole world. And Mili is there, and her guardian angel is there, and all these good guys are there.[93]

SAD ENDING

Dear Mili: An Old Tale has a sad ending—the death of the young heroine. Critics have suggested that Mili's death may be too dark for young children to accept, and parents would do well to shield their children from the story. Writing in *School Library Journal*, critic Patricia Dooley suggested "parents might at least choose to modify or omit the last few lines at bedtime readings."[94] Critic Megan Anderson Bergstrom provided a far harsher analysis of the story, writing in *Mothering* magazine:

A few months after Hans Krasa wrote Brundibar, *Nazis invaded Czechoslovakia. Because Krasa was Jewish, his music was barred from public performances. In spite of this, children living in a Jewish orphanage in the city of Prague performed the opera three times in 1942 before being sent to the Terezin concentration camp. Pictured here is a performance of* Brundibar *at the Knutzen Family Theater in Federal Way, Washington.*

But for children, who look to the text and illustrations for clues to the reality of a story, this is an unexpected and shocking death—what astute kids call a "bad surprise." It is an ending that dashes hopes and daunts courage . . . Although it may have escaped the notice of critics impressed by Sendak's artistic mastery, girls as well as boys need courage. They look to books not only for entertainment and problem-solving skills, but also for "encouragement."[95]

Sendak bristled at the criticism, insisting that death is a part of life, and most children must face the loss of a grandparent, or other close relatives, or even sometimes close friends. Indeed, if the character of Mili is truly based on Anne Frank, Sendak's readers should know that Anne did not survive the Holocaust. The Nazis discovered the Frank family's hiding place. The Franks were sent to a concentration camp, where Anne died just months before liberation by the Allies. Sendak said:

> People have said that *Dear Mili* should be kept from children because it has a fearful ending—because Mili dies. I think it's a book eminently for children. Anyone who thinks that children don't worry, don't ponder, don't obsess about dying, who thinks that Grimm's tale is going to put that thought in their mind, seems to me incredibly naïve. I'll tell you the reaction of the first little girl who saw *Dear Mili*. She did cry, and her mother said, "Are you unhappy because Mili died?" and she said, "No, no." She knew that from the beginning—she knew there was no other way for the book to end. What she was crying about was, why did the rose have to die? Why didn't they put it in water before they went to bed? It's just the pragmatic business of being a child: Does everybody have to die? Couldn't the rose have survived?[96]

BRUNDIBAR

Wilhelm Grimm wrote *Dear Mili: An Old Tale* as a letter to a young girl. The letter remained hidden for 172 years until it surfaced in Germany in 1983 and was made available by its owner for publication as a storybook. In 2003, Sendak discovered another story with a strong Holocaust message and again lent his talents to turn it into a storybook as well as an opera. The story is titled *Brundibar*, a Czech word that means "bumblebee."

The story was written as an opera in 1938 by Czech composer Hans Krasa. It tells the tale of a brother and sister, Pepicek and Aninku, whose mother is ill. To save her life the two children go to a nearby city to buy milk, but they have no money. To raise money for the milk, the children sing in the town square but they are bullied by a hurdy-gurdy (a stringed instrument in which sound is produced by the friction of a rosined wheel turned by a crank against the strings) player named Brundibar who chases them away. The children hide in an alley, where they are befriended by a cat, a sparrow, and a dog, who find other children to help Pepicek and Aninku drive Brundibar away. All the children gather together to sing the finale, which is greeted with enthusiasm by the people of the city who shower them with money. Pepicek and Aninku use the money to buy milk for their mother, who recovers. "It's a sweet tale," said playwright Tony Kushner, who collaborated with Sendak on the project, "but it has a tragic history."[97]

A few months after Krasa wrote the opera, Czechoslovakia was invaded by the Nazis. Krasa was Jewish. As such, his music was barred from public performances. In spite of this, the opera was performed three times in 1942 by the children living in a Jewish orphanage in the city of Prague. When the Nazis learned of the production of the opera, they rounded up the children, the musical conductor, members of the orchestra, and even the stage workers, and sent them to the Terezin concentration camp. Krasa was sent to the camp as well.

Terezin was no ordinary concentration camp. Stories of the horrific conditions at the camps had leaked out and officials from humanitarian agencies such as the International Red Cross demanded to know the truth about the concentration camps. Nazi leader Adolf Hitler wanted to show these groups that the camps' conditions were not so bad, so he established Terezin as a model camp and populated it with the finest Jewish artists, writers, composers,

Did you know...

In 1970, Maurice Sendak was selected as the first American illustrator to win the Hans Christian Andersen Medal, which is awarded each even-numbered year to authors and illustrators of children's literature. The medal, named in honor of the 19th-century author of such stories as "The Ugly Duckling," "The Emperor's New Clothes," and "The Little Mermaid," is awarded by the Switzerland-based International Board on Books for Young People. Other winners of the medal have included Astrid Lindgren of Sweden, who created the Pippi Longstocking series of books, Scott O'Dell, author of *Island of the Blue Dolphins*, and Meindert DeJong, author of several stories that have been illustrated by Sendak.

The award is presented to the winners by the queen of Denmark. It is the most prestigious award in children's literature, and has often been referred to as the "Little Nobel Prize."

and musicians who had been gathered from throughout Europe. Next, he invited diplomats and humanitarian workers to tour Terezin so they could see how well the people were treated, even producing a film of the artists and actors at work. Of course, beneath the surface, Terezin was no different than any of the other camps—the prisoners were doomed to death in the gas chambers. Sendak told an interviewer for National Public Radio:

> It became known as Hitler's favorite camp. He set it up in such a way and he made a film, about how well the children were being treated . . . These rumors were getting out that were frightful, and so he set this up to prove to the Red Cross and the diplomats who were traveling the world to come by and see a show and see how happy everybody was . . . Oh, absolutely they fell for it. The streets were clean, trees were planted, the children were given clean clothes, all the inmates were given clean clothes, everything was swept up.[98]

TIMELESS MESSAGE

In 1943, the young inmates of Terezin staged a production of *Brundibar*, performing the opera 55 times before audiences that included officials from the International Red Cross. Nazi filmmakers included excerpts from the production in a propaganda movie they planned to show to prove how well the Jews were treated. Alas, nearly all the children who performed in the opera did not survive the war. They were sent to the Nazi concentration camp known as Auschwitz, where they died in the gas chambers. Hans Krasa himself died at Auschwitz in 1944.

Coming across the story of Krasa and *Brundibar* "was not a random thing," Sendak told a reporter. "I have a huge collection of books that have to do with the war and the

Holocaust. The story of the opera *Brundibar* and the children performing it in the camp is well known and I had stumbled upon it again and again without connecting myself to it."[99]

As Sendak thought about the story, he knew he had to revive the opera and produce it for the American stage. Sendak said he was particularly moved by the theme of the story of *Brundibar*—the triumph of good over evil. "It's a very simple story, the most basic of fairy tales,"[100] Sendak told *Time* magazine. Kushner added that the story conveys a "timeless message of the necessity to stand up against bullies."[101]

Sendak also resolved to produce a storybook version of *Brundibar*. He enlisted Kushner to write an English language version of the libretto for the opera as well as the story for the book version. For the operatic prodiction, Kushner changed the names of the two children from Aninku and Pepicek to Annette and Little Joe—although the Czech names are used in the storybook version. As for Sendak, his role called for him to design the sets and costumes in the opera and, of course, create the illustrations for the storybook.

One of the main issues for both the book and operatic versions of the story that Sendak and Kushner found themselves facing was how to portray the villain Brundibar. In the opera, Brundibar is supposed to be a teenager—a bit older than Annette and Little Joe, which makes him a menacing figure to the two younger children. Sendak wanted Brundibar to resemble Hitler, the ultimate villain of every Holocaust story. He produced several sketches showing an adult Adolf Hitler comically grinding his hurdy-gurdy, but Kushner decided that the image of Hitler menacing young children would burden parents with too many questions to answer when they read the book to their sons and daughters. Next, Sendak portrayed Brundibar as Hitler wearing a clown costume. Again, Kushner protested. "Was it right to play hide and seek with Hitler's visage, an icon of human evil?" Kushner asked.[102]

And so, Sendak finally drew Brundibar as a younger version of Hitler, making him a teenager but giving him a cartoonish mustache and dressing him in a clownish uniform that suggested more of an image of Napoleon Bonaparte than Adolf Hitler. Despite the decision to draw the villain as someone other than Hitler, Sendak does include some references to the Holocaust in the book. For example, a banner stretched across a page resembles a sign that greeted the inmates as they arrived at Auschwitz. The pages also include images of townspeople wearing yellow stars of David, the international symbol of the Jewish people. During the Holocaust, European Jews were ordered by the Nazis to wear the six-pointed stars sewn into their overcoats so that they could be easily identified. Sendak also uses the pages of the book to point out that others besides Jews were the victims of the Holocaust. In the children's home, a crucifix hangs over the bed of the ill mother. She is treated, though, by a Jewish doctor who proclaims "Mazel Tov" when Aninku and Pepicek bring home the milk. "Mazel Tov" is an expression in Yiddish—a language spoken by European Jews—that means "congratulations." Finally, Sendak and Kushner have included a note on the book jacket informing readers that Krasa died at Auschwitz.

In 2003, *Brundibar* was performed by the Chicago Opera Theater. Since then, it has been staged in other cities as well. When the opera premiered in Chicago, a member of the audience was Ela Stein Weissberger, one of the few survivors from the Terezin cast. Back at Terezin, Weissberger had been selected to play the role of the cat. Weissberger told a news reporter that the opera was the only bright moment in the lives of the young children imprisoned at Terezin. She said, "With Brundibar, we forgot hunger, we forgot where we were."[103]

In 2005, the Jewish Museum in New York, pictured here, featured an exhibit of Maurice Sendak's artwork. The exhibit covered the breadth of Sendak's career as a storybook author and illustrator as well as a set and costume designer.

8

Still Scaring Children

WHEN MAURICE SENDAK ILLUSTRATED Ruth Krauss's book, *A Hole is to Dig*, Krauss was already a well-established author of children's storybooks while Sendak was, of course, just getting his start. Four years before Sendak illustrated *A Hole is to Dig*, Krauss wrote a storybook titled *Bears*. The book, which contains just 27 words, shows bears "on the stairs . . . under chairs"[104] as well as performing other everyday tasks, such as washing their hair, or giving stares toward one another, or acting like millionaires. When the book was first published in 1948, the drawings of the bears were provided by illustrator Phyllis Rowand.

In 2005, Sendak was asked to illustrate a new version of *Bears*. This time, he would not be able to consult with Krauss—she died in 1993. Still, Sendak wanted to pay tribute to Krauss and her husband, Dave Johnson, who gave him his start as a storybook illustrator and helped him develop his talents. And so he decided to insert Max from *Where the Wild Things Are* into the new version. According to Sendak, in 1960 as he conceived the idea for *Where the Wild Things Are* as well as many of his other storybooks, he was making regular trips to the Rowayton, Connecticut, home of Krauss and Johnson, where they helped him sketch out his early ideas for his stories. In an interview on National Public Radio, Sendak recalled:

> I was just this hopeless, naïve kid. But I had a lucky life because I had them very early in my career, in my early twenties, and they adopted me, Ruth and Dave, that is . . . What I got from Ruth and Dave, a kind of fierce honesty, to not let the kid down, to not let the kid get punished, to not suffer the child to be dealt with in a boring, simpering, crushing-of-the-spirit kind of way.[105]

Actually, Sendak gives Krauss and Johnson credit for more than just spiritual guidance. In *Where the Wild Things Are*, a turning point in the story is when Max orders the "rumpus" to begin. It was Johnson, Sendak said, who recommended the word "rumpus" to describe the wild party in the forest.

In the new version of *Bears*, the pages continue to show bears on the stairs and under chairs and so on, but this time the story commences when Max's jealous dog kidnaps his teddy bear. Max, wearing his familiar wolf costume, spends the rest of the book chasing his dog and teddy around the world of the bears. The book ends with Max retrieving his teddy bear and taking it with him to bed. He also invites his dog to sleep in the bed. The final scene shows Max, the dog, and the teddy bear curled up in bed, but there is something of a pained expression on the teddy bear's face—suggesting that the bear is not altogether happy with the way things turned out. The story is, of course, a bit more complicated than the first version by Krauss and Rowand; nevertheless, Sendak believes today's young readers are looking for more than a book with words that accompany pictures. As he has believed for a long time, Sendak insists that the text and the illustrations share equal duty in telling the story. He said:

> The difference between what I did and what Phyllis did is a generational thing. What she did was literally take what Ruth said, "Bears on the stairs," and drew them on the stairs. Then I come in a generation later, and I have to make a story on top of a story. It's not enough that it just be what she did. I need something more. Like so much of *Wild Things* is not in the language, the story continues in the pictures. It's like an accompaniment to the text. You're not just—I don't like the word "illustrating." I like the word "picture-making," because if you're just illustrating, it means you're like an echo of the text. Who needs it?[106]

Parents who choose to read Sendak's books to their children at bedtime know that he often presents stories with socially-relevant themes; however that was not the case with *Bears*. Sendak said he wanted *Bears* to be nothing more than pure fun—the way Krauss intended the book to be more than a half-century ago. That is why he chose to illustrate *Bears* in crayon—so that the book would have a roughness of the images, as though they were drawn during playtime.

The decision to insert Max into *Bears* represents a departure for Sendak, who for decades has resisted offers from publishers to insert Max into sequels of *Where the Wild Things Are*. Sendak believed Max's story was told in *Where the Wild Things Are*, and there was no reason to find new adventures for him. He departed from that position, he said, because *Bears* "was Ruth Krauss's book."[107] He added:

> Max comes in because a lot of the work I did on Wild Things was up at Rowayton, and I was having a problem with the book. It was a very difficult book. It was my first picture book. So I feel as though Max was born in Rowayton and that he was the love child of me, Ruth and Dave. And so when I got to do this one, I'm thinking, what is the story? What is the other story? And it had to be Max. There was no question it had to be Max. This is the last time this will ever happen in my life, that this kind of experience will occur, where I can be back with them [Krauss and Johnson]."[108]

IMPACT ON AMERICAN CULTURE

His willingness to illustrate a new version of *Bears* shows that as he approaches the age of 80, Sendak has no plans to slow down. Indeed, Sendak said he intends to continue illustrating and writing books for many years to come. He also wants to teach so that he can help young illustrators get their starts. He told National Public Radio:

> I want to be a mentor. I want to be Ruth and Dave. That's my goal in life . . . I don't know how long I'm going to live, and so one of the things I want to do is, this big gorilla head that's stuffed with experience, I want to give it away before I'm gone. I want to give it away to young artists who are as vehement and passionate about their lives and work as I was and am.[109]

Although Sendak is still a working illustrator, he has

clearly earned recognition as something more than a commercial artist who simply provides pictures for storybooks. In recent years, his work has been recognized as examples of important American art. Therefore, he has made the leap from book illustrator to an artist and writer whose work has made an impact on American culture.

Did you know...

Maurice Sendak is a life-long fan of Mickey Mouse. Both Sendak and Mickey were born in 1928. Sendak has filled his art studio in Connecticut with all manner of Mickey Mouse memorabilia—from clocks to toys to banks. He has collected so much memorabilia, in fact, that many of the items have been placed on display in the Maurice Sendak Gallery of the Rosenbach Museum in Philadelphia. In 2005, Sendak told National Public Radio:

> I fell in love with Mickey, because I went to the movies . . . with my sister [Natalie] and brother [Jack], and you had a double feature and a cartoon in the middle, so you were there for hours out of the hands of your parents. And there's the cartoon, and when I saw the cartoon, I went into a frenzy. I remember my sister saying, "We knew it was coming, and Jackie would grab you by one arm and I would grab you by the other arm and you would have a seizure." First the big head would appear with radiant lights coming out of it. Remember that? And I adored him and I still do. I adore him from then.

Sendak said he dreamed of becoming an animator for the Disney studio in California. Sendak said he wrote to studio founder Walt Disney asking for a job. "He never wrote back," Sendak said.

In 2005, the Jewish Museum in New York featured an exhibit of Sendak's artwork, covering the breadth of his career as a storybook author and illustrator as well as set and costume designer. The exhibit was culled from some 10,000 pieces of Sendak artwork owned by Rosenbach Museum and Library in Philadelphia, which maintains a Sendak gallery. In fact, Sendak has made Rosenbach Museum and Library the official repository of his work. The gallery is housed in the "Sendak Building" on the museum grounds. It opened in 2003.

An exhibit at the Rosenbach Museum and Library shows how *Where the Wild Things Are* evolved from an idea in Sendak's sketchbook into a published storybook. One of the pieces on display in the gallery is a sketchbook that includes the original concept for a book about wild horses. The exhibit also includes Sendak's journal entries on what he thought about his ideas. For example, on April 16, 1963, he wrote in his journal:

> The story bogs simply, it loses "picture" book quality and gets too literary, so back to 1955 picture version. Keep simple and humorous and keep allegory under control.[110]

A few weeks later, he had this to say about Max's experience with the wild horses:

> *"I'm as hungry as a horse," the boy tells his mother.*
> *"A wild horse," says his mother.*
> Abandon!!!! Dreadful story![111]

SENDAK'S CONTRIBUTIONS TO LITERATURE

The display at the Jewish Museum as well as the Rosenbach's gallery and extensive collection serves as a testament to Sendak's long and productive career in children's literature. In 2003, his full body of work was examined during a program sponsored by the American Library Association and the Association for Library Services for Children at the Cambridge Public Library in Massachusetts. Events that occurred during the symposium included a performance of *Really Rosie*, an exhibit of artwork by local school children who were assigned to provide their own illustrations for Sendak's stories, and a lecture by Sendak attended by some 1,200 librarians.

While Sendak's artwork is displayed in museums and analyzed for its impact on American culture, critics are also taking a new look at his writing. No longer is he accused of introducing socially-relevant themes to children who are too young to understand them. Indeed, now he rarely hears critics complain that he is frightening little children. During the Sendak symposium at Cambridge, author Gregory Maguire spoke about Sendak's impact on children's literature. Reprinted in the magazine *Horn Book*, Maguire said that before Sendak started writing children's storybooks, authors tried to shield young children from the darker side of life. Authors of storybooks, Maguire said, harbored the "notion of childhood as paradise,"[112] and that

> in one form or another, that vain and perhaps decadent notion persisted from its . . . Peter-Pan-ish, Pooh-ish heyday well into the 1960s. With the world going to hell in a handbasket at twenty-year intervals, it's easy to understand why adults would cling to their imprecise recollections of childhood as a time of untroubled joy . . .
>
> Lots and lots of good children's books were written in those decades. If any light was shed on the peril and the promise of human existence, however, it was only rarely in picture books. Except for the works of Beatrix Potter and . . . a few others, picture books generally preserved the sanctity of

Maurice Sendak (right) is almost 80 years old, but as pictured here at the Childrens Museum of Manhattan in New York City, he continues to mentor children, particularly those who are interested in illustrating their own books. He also intends to illustrate and write books for many more years to come.

the nursery, where the green baize door to the downstairs closed out anything unsuitable that might vex the impressionably young mind.

What Sendak contributed, before, during, and since *Where the Wild Things Are*, is a juvenile grammar of narrative and image capable of conveying the anxiety and adventure and

potential safety of the mortal world—a grammar easily deci-
pherable by a child too young to read.[113]

"THE CREATIVE POWER OF HUMAN BEINGS"

Sendak makes his home in the countryside near Ridgefield,
Connecticut. He never married, and his sole companion is a
German shepherd named Herman, named after Herman
Melville—the novelist who has provided Sendak with so
much inspiration. He enjoys sleeping late, working into the
early hours of the morning, watching television, and listen-
ing to Mozart as he draws.

Certainly, he does not intend to abandon his practice of
bringing socially-relevant themes to the attention of young
American readers. In 2006, a production of *Brundibar* was
planned for the Broadway stage in New York City. Since the
opera is brief—it spans less than an hour—it was performed
with another brief Hans Krasa opera in which Sendak has
designed the sets and costumes and Kushner has provided an
English language libretto. The opera is titled *Comedy on the
Bridge*, and tells the story of a young couple and a befuddled
schoolmaster who find themselves stuck in the middle of a
bridge, separating two opposing armies. Kushner told *Playbill* magazine, "Both shows are a testament to the creative
power of human beings [to] even in dark times, to turn ugli-
ness into music."[114]

Certainly, one of the most creative human beings of the
20th and 21st centuries has been Maurice Sendak, who rose
from a sickly childhood and a humble family life into one of
the most acclaimed storybook authors and artists in the history of children's literature. He has taken the storybook
medium and introduced many themes that adults thought
children might have troubling facing: fear, loneliness, prejudice, war, and death, among them. But children seem to be

able to absorb the books' lessons. Perhaps they are better able to accept those themes as they learn to read and find books without happy endings. For as long as he is able to take pencil in hand and sketch an idea onto a drawing pad, Sendak will continue producing books the only way he knows how. In 2006, Sendak is planning to publish a pop-up storybook. When a reporter asked him to talk about the book, he would only disclose, "The story line is scaring children, my favorite subject."[115]

1 Mike Capuzzo, "Sendak's Back, Startling Adults Anew," *Knight-Ridder/Tribune News Service*, September 28, 1993.

2 "Maurice Sendak Talks About His New Book, Homelessness," *All Things Considered*, National Public Radio, October 30, 1993.

3 Brian Alderson, "Children's Books; Children Who Live In Boxes," *The New York Times*, November 14, 1993, *http://query.nytimes.com/gst/fullpage.html?res=9F0CE3D6123AF937A25752C1A965958260.*

4 Ibid.

5 "Maurice Sendak Talks About His New Book, Homelessness."

6 Brian Alderson, "Children Who Live in Boxes."

7 "Where the Wild Things Roam," *Time* Vol. 142, No. 26, December 20, 1993, 64.

8 Ibid.

9 "Maurice Sendak Talks About His New Book, Homelessness."

10 Selma G. Lanes, *The Art of Maurice Sendak* (New York, NY: Abradale Press, 1980), 12.

11 "Artist, Writer and Designer Maurice Sendak," *Fresh Air*, October 30, 2003, *www.npr.org/templates/story/story.php?storyId=1484744.*

12 Lanes, *The Art of Maurice Sendak*, 12.

13 Ibid, 13.

14 Ibid.

15 Ibid, 16.

16 Laurie Lanzen Harris, ed., "Maurice Sendak," *Biography Today Author Series* Vol. 2 (Detroit, MI: Omnigraphics Inc., 1996), 123.

17 Lanes, *The Art of Maurice Sendak*, 29.

18 Ibid, 33.

19 Ibid.

20 Ibid, 34.

21 Ann Evory and Linda Metzger, ed., *Contemporary Authors New Revision Series* Vol. 11 (Detroit, MI: Gale Research Co., 1984), 459.

22 Lanes, *The Art of Maurice Sendak*, 43.

23 Ibid.

24 Ibid, 63.

25 Ibid, 64.

26 Ibid, 64–65.

27 Ibid, 65–66.

28 Ibid, 66.

29 Ibid, 67.

30 Maurice Sendak, *Where the Wild Things Are* (New York, NY: HarperCollins, 1988).

31 Ibid.

32 Lanes, *The Art of Maurice Sendak*, 93.

33 Evory and Metzger, ed., *Contemporary Authors New Revision Series* Vol. 11, 460.

34 Ibid.

35 Ibid.

36 Saul Braun, "Sendak Raises the Shade on Childhood," *New York Times Sunday Magazine*, June 7, 1970, 40.

37 Ibid.

38 Ibid.

39 Maurice Sendak, *In the Night Kitchen* (New York: Harper & Row, 1970).

40 *Questions to An Artist Who is Also an Author: A Conversation Between Maurice Sendak and Virginia Haviland* (Washington, DC: Library of Congress, 1972), 270.

41 Ibid.

42 Ibid.

43 Maurice Sendak, *Outside Over There* (New York, NY: Harper & Row, 1981).

44 Roger Sutton, "An Interview with Maurice Sendak," *The Horn Book Magazine* (November–December 2003), *www.hbook.com/publications/magazine/articles/nov03_sendak_sutton.asp.*

45 Evory and Metzger, ed., *Contemporary Authors New Revision Series* Vol. 11, 461.

46 Ibid.

47 Ibid, 461–462.

48 Leonard S. Marcus, ed., *Dear Genius: The Letters of Ursula Nordstrom* (New York, NY: HarperCollins, 1999), 344.

49 Ibid, 326.

50 Ibid.

51 Susan Lampert Smith, "A Parental Prerogative . . . Banned Books List Continues to Grow," *Wisconsin State Journal*, September 28, 1993.

52 Herbert N. Foerstel, *Banned in the USA: A Reference Guide to Book Censorship in Schools and Public Libraries* (Westport, CT: Greenwood Press, 1994), 201.

53 Ibid.

54 Shelton L. Root, "In the Night Kitchen," *Elementary English*, February 1971, reprinted in Amy Sonheim, *Maurice Sendak* (New York, NY: Twayne Publishers, 1991), 13–14.

55 David S. Davis, "Wrong Recipe Used *In the Night Kitchen*," Elementary English, February 1971, reprinted in Amy Sonheim, *Maurice Sendak* (New York, NY: Twayne Publishers, 1991), 14.

56 Martha Shirk, "Gloomy Relatives Inspired 'Wild Things,'" *St. Louis Post-Dispatch*, December 4, 1989, reprinted in Sonheim, *Maurice Sendak*, 14.

57 "The Most Frequently Challenged Books of 2004," American Library Association, *www.ala.org/ala/oif/bannedbooksweek/challengedbanned/challengedbanned.htm.*

58 Ellen Handler Spitz, *Inside Picture Books* (New Haven, CT: Yale University Press, 1999), 60.

59 Ibid, 64.

60 Judith Levine, *Harmful to Minors* (Minneapolis, MN: University of Minnesota Press, 2002), 13.

61 Ibid, 13–14.

62 Ibid, 142–143.

63 Maurice Sendak, "Why Mickey Wears No Pants," *Los Angeles Times Book Review*, June 16, 1991, 1.

64 Lanes, *The Art of Maurice Sendak*, 189.

65 Marcus, ed., *Dear Genius: The Letters of Ursula Nordstrom*, 334–335.

66 Sendak, "Why Mickey Wears No Pants,"1.

67 Lanes, *The Art of Maurice Sendak*, 110.

68 Ibid, 185.

69 Ibid, 85.

70 Maurice Sendak, *Higglety Pigglety Pop! or There Must be More to Life* (New York, NY: Harper & Row, 1967), 3.

71 William Zinsser, ed., *Worlds of Childhood: The Art and Craft of Writing for Children* (Boston, MA: Houghton Mifflin Co., 1990), 58.

72 Lanes, *The Art of Maurice Sendak*, 96.

73 Sendak, *Where the Wild Things Are*.

74 Zinsser, ed., *Worlds of Childhood: The Art and Craft of Writing for Children*, 60.

75 Howard W. Reeves, ed., *Wings of an Artist: Children's Book Illustrators Talk About Their Art* (New York, NY: Harry N. Abrams Inc., 1999), 26.

76 Lanes, *The Art of Maurice Sendak*, 193.

77 Ibid, 232.

78 Ibid, 179–182.

79 Ibid, 182.

80 Ibid, 88.

81 Ibid.

82 Zinsser, ed., *Worlds of Childhood: The Art and Craft of Writing for Children*, 52–53.

83 "Interview with Maurice Sendak," *Backstage at Lincoln Center*, *www.pbs.org/lflc/dec17/sendak.htm*.

84 Tony Kushner, *The Art of Maurice Sendak: 1980 to the Present* (New York, NY: Harry N. Abrams Inc., 2003), 86.

85 Sarah H. Wright, "Sendak Sketches a Life in Children's Art," Massachusetts Institute of Technology News Office, April 9, 2003, *http://web.mit.edu/newsoffice/2003/sendack-0409.html*.

86 Kushner, *The Art of Maurice Sendak: 1980 to the Present*, 92.

87 Maurice Sendak, "The Nutcracker and the Mouse King," *http://users.htcomp.net/weis/nutcrintro.html*.

88 Kushner, *The Art of Maurice Sendak: 1980 to the Present*, 129–130.

89 Ibid, 136.

90 Ibid, 142.

91 Ibid.

92 Terry Gross, *All I Did Was Ask: Conversations with Writers, Actors*, Musicians and Artists (New York, NY: Hyperion, 2004), 343.

93 Zinsser, ed., *Worlds of Childhood: The Art and Craft of Writing for Children*, 54.

94 Patricia Dooley, "Dear Mili: An Old Tale," *School Library Journal*, November 1, 1988.

95 Megan Anderson Bergstrom, "*Dear Mili*," *Mothering*, Spring 1990,

www.findarticles.com/p/articles/
mi_m0838/is_n55/ai_8898303.

96 Zinsser, ed., *Worlds of Childhood:
The Art and Craft of Writing for
Children*, 54–55.

97 Kushner, *The Art of Maurice
Sendak: 1980 to the Present*, 206.

98 "Artist, Writer and Designer
Maurice Sendak."

99 Sally Lodge, "Brundibar: A
Collaboration with Remarkable
Roots," *Publishers Weekly* Vol.
250, No. 43, October 27, 2003,
26.

100 Heather Won Tesoriero, "Where
Young Things Are: Maurice
Sendak Revives and Lightens a
Children's Opera First Performed
in a Nazi Concentration Camp,"
Time Vol. 161, No. 22, June 2,
2003, 79.

101 Ibid.

102 Kushner, *The Art of Maurice
Sendak: 1980 to the Present*, 210.

103 Tesoriero, "Where Young Things
Are: Maurice Sendak Revives and
Lightens a Children's Opera First
Performed in a Nazi
Concentration Camp," 79.

104 Jennifer M. Brown, "The Rumpus
Goes On: Max, Maurice Sendak
and a Clan of Bears Pay Tribute

to a Lifelong Mentorship,"
Publishers Weekly, April 18,
2005.

105 "Maurice Sendak Discusses His
Work," Weekend Edition,
National Public Radio, June 4,
2005.

106 Ibid.

107 Ibid

108 Ibid.

109 Ibid.

110 Susan D. Haas, "Maurice Sendak:
Forty Years on the Wild Side,"
The Morning Call, Allentown,
September 27, 2003.

111 Ibid.

112 Gregory Maguire, "A Sendak
Appreciation," *Horn Book* Vol.
79, No. 6, November 1, 2002,
667.

113 Ibid.

114 Ernio Hernandez, "Kushner and
Sendak's Brundibar and Comedy
on the Bridge Added to Yale Rep
Lineup Before NY," *Playbill*,
August 31, 2005,
www.playbill.com/news/arti-
cle/94844.html.

115 "Maurice Sendak Discusses His
Work."

1928 Maurice Sendak born in Brooklyn, New York, June 10, 1928.

1946 Graduates Lafayette High School, finds a job decorating department store windows.

1949 Designs and builds mechanical toys with his brother Jack Sendak. Hired to decorate the display windows at F.A.O. Schwarz toy store in Manhattan, New York.

1950 Assigned by book editor Ursula Nordstrom to illustrate *The Wonderful Farm* by Marcel Aymé.

1952 Illustrates *A Hole is to Dig* by Ruth Krauss.

1956 Writes and illustrates *Kenny's Window*.

1963 Writes and illustrates *Where the Wild Things Are*.

1964 Wins the Caldecott Medal for *Where the Wild Things Are*.

1970 Writes and illustrates *In the Night Kitchen*; wins the Hans Christian Andersen International Medal.

1972 A librarian in Louisiana paints a diaper of Mickey in the pages of *In the Night Kitchen*, beginning a long-running battle against censorship of the book.

1980 *Where the Wild Things Are* debuts as an opera. Sendak designs costumes and sets for *The Magic Flute*.

1983 Designs sets and costumes and writes the libretto for a production of the ballet *The Nutcracker*.

1988 Illustrates the Wilhelm Grimm story *Dear Mili: An Old Tale*.

1993 Writes and illustrates *We Are All in the Dumps With Jack and Guy*.

2003 Designs sets and costumes for *Brundibar* and publishes the story in a book version.

2005 Illustrates a new version of *Bears* by Ruth Krauss.

A HOLE IS TO DIG

A Hole is to Dig is the book by Ruth Krauss that launched Maurice Sendak's career as an illustrator. Krauss asked young children to answer some simple questions, and learned that hands are to hold, buttons are to keep people warm, dogs are to kiss people, and a hole is to dig.

KENNY'S WINDOW

Kenny's Window was the first book written and illustrated by Maurice Sendak. The book tells the story of a boy who awakens from a dream and embarks on adventures to answer questions posed to him by a four-legged rooster. When Kenny has answered all of the questions, he is offered a trip to a magical garden. He turns down the offer and instead returns home.

THE SIGN ON ROSIE'S DOOR

In *The Sign on Rosie's Door*, Rosie and her friends must find a way to endure a boring summer day. Rosie decides to dress up in her mother's clothes and put on a show.

WHERE THE WILD THINGS ARE

Where the Wild Things Are established Maurice Sendak as a major contributor to children's literature. The story follows a mischievous little boy as he defies his mother, leaves home, sails across an ocean, and discovers a land of hideous beasts whom he tames and becomes their king.

HIGGLETY PIGGLETY POP! OR THERE MUST BE MORE TO LIFE

In the pages of *Higglety Pigglety Pop! or There Must be More to Life*, a dog named Jennie decides to see what life is like away from home. She becomes the nanny of a bratty baby, then saves the child from a lion. As a reward, Jennie is given the lead role in a musical play.

IN THE NIGHT KITCHEN

In the Night Kitchen begins with Mickey being awakened by a racket in the kitchen downstairs. He investigates and finds three roly-poly bakers preparing the next day's bread. When they mistake him for a bottle of milk, Mickey makes his escape by fashioning an airplane out of bread dough.

OUTSIDE OVER THERE

The story of *Outside Over There* was inspired by the Lindbergh baby kidnapping and murder. Maurice Sendak has turned the tale into a coming-of-age story in which a girl is forced to grow up and rescue her baby sister from goblins.

DEAR MILI: AN OLD TALE

The story of *Dear Mili: An Old Tale* was written by Wilhelm Grimm in 1816 and remained unpublished until Maurice Sendak discovered it 172 years later. Grimm wrote about a mother who sends her young daughter into the forest to escape a war; Sendak turned Grimm's tale into a Holocaust story, suggesting that Mili was escaping from a Nazi concentration camp.

THE NUTCRACKER

Maurice Sendak collaborated with Kent Stowell, the artistic director of the Pacific Northwest Ballet company, on a new version of the ballet *The Nutcracker* in which a young girl is saved from the clutches of the Mouse King by a prince who has been turned into a toy nutcracker; following the premier of the ballet Sendak produced a storybook version.

WE ARE ALL IN THE DUMPS WITH JACK AND GUY

Maurice Sendak was inspired to write *We Are All in the Dumps With Jack and Guy* after he saw a homeless boy sleeping in a box in a wealthy California neighborhood; he borrows Mother Goose rhymes to tell the story of the rescue of a little boy and kittens from the clutches of evil rats.

BRUNDIBAR

Based on an opera by the Czech composer Hans Krasa, *Brundibar* tells the story of two young children who overcome the taunts of a bully. Krasa's opera was performed by young inmates of a Nazi concentration camp; as such, Maurice Sendak has given the story a Holocaust theme.

BEARS

The book *Bears* by Ruth Krauss helped children learn simple words by putting bears through everyday tasks; when Maurice Sendak re-illustrated the story, he drew the character of Max from *Where the Wild Things Are* on a quest to rescue his teddy bear from a jealous dog.

WRITTEN AND ILLUSTRATED

1956 *Kenny's Window*

1957 *Very Far Away*

1959 *The Acrobat*

1660 *The Sign on Rosie's Door*

1962 *The Nutshell Library*

1963 *Where the Wild Things Are*

1965 *Hector Protector and As I Went over the Water: Two Nursery Rhymes*

1967 *Higglety Pigglety Pop! or There Must Be More to Life*

1970 *In the Night Kitchen*; *Ten Little Rabbits: A Counting Book with Mino the Magician*

1971 *Pictures by Maurice Sendak*; *Fantasy Drawings*; *The Magician: A Counting Book*

1975 *Maurice Sendak's Really Rosie*

1976 *Some Swell Pup: or, Are You Sure You Want a Dog?* with Matthew Margolis

1977 *Seven Little Monsters*

1981 *Outside Over There*

1993 *We're All in the Dumps With Jack and Guy*

ILLUSTRATED

1947 *Atomics for the Millions* by M.L. Eidinoff and Hyman Ruchlis

1951 *Good Shabbos, Everybody!* by Robert Garvey; *The Wonderful Farm* by Marcel Aymé

1952 *A Hole is to Dig: A First Book of Definitions* by Ruth Krauss; *Maggie Rose: Her Birthday Christmas* by Ruth Sawyer

1953 *The Giant Story* by Beatrice S. de Regniers; *Hurry Home, Candy* by Meindert De Jong; *Shadrach* by Meindert DeJong; *A Very Special House* by Ruth Krauss

1954 *Happy Hanukah, Everybody* by Hyman Chanover; *I'll be You and You'll Be Me* by Ruth Krauss; *The Tin Fiddle* by Edward Tripp; *Magic Pictures* by Marcel Aymé; *Mrs. Piggle-Wiggle's Farm* by Betty MacDonald; *The Wheel on the School* by Meindert DeJong

1955 *Charlotte and the White Horse* by Ruth Krauss; *The Little Cow and the Turtle* by Meindert De Jong; *Singing Family of the*

Cumberlands by Jean Ritchie; *What Can You Do with a Shoe?* by Beatrice S. de Regniers; *Seven Little Stories on Big Subjects* by Gladys Baker Bond

1956 *The Happy Rain* by Jack Sendak; *The House of Sixty Fathers* by Meindert De Jong; *I Want to Paint My Bathroom Blue* by Ruth Krauss

1957 *Birthday Party* by Ruth Krauss; *Circus Girl* by Jack Sendak; *You Can't Get There From Here* by Ogden Nash; *Little Bear* by Else Holmelund Minarik

1958 *Along Came a Dog* by Meindert DeJong; *No Fighting, No Biting* by Else Holmelund Minarik; *Somebody Else's Nut Tree and Other Tales from Children* by Ruth Krauss; *What Do You Say, Dear? A Book of Manners for All Occasions* by Sesyle Joslyn

1959 *Father Bear Comes Home* by Else Holmelund Minarik; *The Moon Jumpers* by Janice Udry; *Seven Tales* by Hans Christian Andersen

1960 *Dwarf Long-Nose* by Wilhelm Hauff; *Little Bear's Friend* by Else Holmelund Minarik; *Open House for Butterflies* by Ruth Krauss

1961 *Let's Be Enemies* by Janice Udry; *The Tale of Gockel, Hinkel, and Gackeliah* by Clemens Brentano; *Little Bear's Visit* by Else Holmelund Minarik; *What Do You Do, Dear?* by Sesyle Joslyn

1962 *Schoolmaster Whackwell's Wonderful Sons* by Clemens Brentano; *Mr. Rabbit and the Lovely Present* by Charlotte Zolotow; *The Singing Hill* by Meindert DeJong

1963 *Nikolenka's Childhood* by Leo Tolstoy; *She Loves Me, She Loves Me Not* by Robert Keeshan

1964 *The Bat-Poet* by Randall Jarrell; *How Little Lori Visited Times Square* by Amos Vogel; *Pleasant Fieldmouse* by Jan Wahl; *Little Stories* by Gladys Baker Bond

1965 *Lullabies and Night Songs* edited by William Engvick; *The Animal Family* by Randall Jarrell

1966 *Zlateh The Goat and Other Stories* by Isaac Bashevis Singer

1967 *The Golden Key* by George MacDonald; *Poems from William Blake's Songs of Innocence* by William Blake

1968 *The Big Green Book* by Robert Graves; *Griffin and the Minor Canon* by Frank Stockton; *A Kiss for Little Bear* by Else Holmelund Minarik

1969 *The Light Princess* by George MacDonald

1971 *The Bee-man of Orn* by Frank Stockton; *Sarah's Room* by Doris Orgel

1973 *The Juniper Tree and Other Tales from Grimm* by Jacob Grimm and Wilhelm Grimm

1974 *Fortunia: A Tale by Mme. D'Aulnoy* by Marie Catherine Jumelle de Berneville

1976 *Fly by Night* by Randall Jarrell

1978 *King Grisley-Beard: A Tale from the Brothers Grimm* by Jacob and Wilhelm Grimm

1983 *Kleist: A Biography* by Joachim Maass

1984 *The Nutcracker* by E.T.A. Hoffman

1985 *In Grandpa's House* by Philip Sendak

The Cunning Little Vixen by Rudolf Tesnohlidek

1988 *Dear Mili: An Old Tale* by Wilhelm Grim; *The Children's Books of Randall Jarrell* by Jerome Griswald with Garth Williams

1992 *I Saw Esau: The Schoolchild's Pocketbook* by Iona and Peter Opie

1995 *The Miami Giant* by Arthur Yorkins

1996 *Pierre; or, the Ambiguities* by Herman Melville; *Penthesilia: A Tragic Drama* by Heinrich von Kleist

1999 *Swine Lake* by James Marshall

2003 *Brundibar* by Tony Kushner

2005 *Bears* by Ruth Krauss

MUSICALS, OPERAS, AND BALLETS

1975 *Really Rosie*, with Carole King: sets, costumes and libretto

1980 *Where the Wild Things Are* [opera version], with Oliver Knussen: sets, costumes and libretto; *The Magic Flute*: sets and costumes

1981 *The Cunning Little Vixen*: sets and costumes

1982 *The Love for Three Oranges*: sets and costumes

1983 *The Cunning Little Vixen*: sets and costumes; *The Nutcracker*: sets, costumes and libretto

1984 *Higglety Pigglety Pop! or There Must Be More to Life*, with Oliver Knussen: sets, costumes and libretto

1986 *L'Enfant et le Sortileges*: sets and costumes; *L'Heure Espagnole*: sets and costumes; *Renard*: sets and costumes; *The Goose from Cairo*: sets and costumes

1989 *Idomeno*: sets and costumes

1996 *Hänsel und Gretel*: sets and costumes

1997 *Where the Wild Things Are* [ballet vesion]: sets, costumes and libretto

2001 *A Selection*: sets and costumes

2003 *Brundibar*, with Tony Kushner: sets and costumes

2005 *Comedy on the Bridge*, with Tony Kushner: sets and costumes

KENNY

Maurice Sendak based the character of Kenny in *Kenny's Window* on a boy he read about in a book written by a child psychologist. Kenny is the first of many characters developed by Sendak who find a way to triumph over life's obstacles.

ROSIE

Rosie is the main character of *The Sign on Rosie's Door* and its musical version, *Really Rosie*. Maurice Sendak started drawing Rosie when he was a child; she was a neighborhood girl who enjoyed entertaining her friends by playacting.

MAX

The boy in the wolf suit chases the dog, threatens to eat his mother, and runs away from home, but once he tames the wild things he discovers there is no place like home. Max reappears in Maurice Sendak's version of the Ruth Krauss book *Bears*, helping tell the story of why bears can be found on the stairs, under chairs, and acting like millionaires.

JENNIE

The main character of *Higglety Pigglety Pop! or There Must be More to Life*, Maurice Sendak based the character of Jennie on his terrier, Jennie, who had been his constant companion for 14 years before her death in 1967.

MICKEY

Mickey is one of Maurice Sendak's most controversial characters because he spends much of the story in the nude. Children who saw the pictures did not seem to mind. They concentrated more on the little boy's adventures escaping from the bakers and finding milk in the Milky Way.

IDA

Ida is fooled by the goblins that kidnap her baby sister by replacing her with an ice sculpture. To find her sister, Ida must fall out of her window into a land "outside over there," where she finds the baby and exposes the goblins as being babies themselves.

MILI

Maurice Sendak based the character of Mili on Anne Frank, the teenager whose famous diary tells how her family hid from the Nazis in an Amsterdam attic during World War II. In *Dear Mili: An Old Tale*, Mili is reunited with her mother at the end of the story but, like Anne Frank, she dies at the end.

JACK AND GUY

The two heroes of *We Are All in the Dumps With Jack and Guy* at first turn their backs on the little boy who is kidnapped by rats, but after losing in a rigged card game Jack and Guy rescue the child.

PEPICEK AND ANINKU

The two young children at the center of the book and opera *Brundibar*, Pepicek and Aninku enlist the aid of a cat, dog and sparrow to drive off the bully Brundibar. With Brundibar gone, the children are showered with money when they sing in the town square. They use the money to buy milk for their ill mother.

1952 *A Hole is to Dig* receives *New York Times* Best Illustrated Book Award.

1954 *I'll Be You and You Be Me* receives *New York Times* Best Illustrated Book Award; *A Very Special House* is awarded Caldecott Medal runner-up by the American Library Association.

1956 *I Want To Paint My Bathroom Blue* receives *New York Times* Best Illustrated Book Award.

1957 *The Birthday Party* receives *New York Times* Best Illustrated Book Award.

1958 *What Do You Say, Dear?* receives *New York Times* Best Illustrated Book Award.

1959 *Father Bear Comes Home* receives *New York Times* Best Illustrated Book Award; *What Do You Say, Dear?* is awarded Caldecott Medal runner-up.

1960 *Open House For Butterflies* receives *New York Times* Best Illustrated Book Award.

1962 *The Singing Hill* receives *New York Times* Best Illustrated Book Award; *Little Bear's Visit* is awarded Caldecott Medal runner-up.

1963 *Where the Wild Things Are* receives *New York Times* Best Illustrated Book Award; *Mr. Rabbit and the Lovely Present* is awarded Caldecott Medal runner-up.

1964 *The Bat-Poet* receives *New York Times* Best Illustrated Book Award; *Where the Wild Things Are* receives Caldecott Medal.

1965 *The Animal Family* receives *New York Times* Best Illustrated Book Award.

1966 *Zlateh the Goat and Other Stories* receives *New York Times* Best Illustrated Book Award.

1968 *A Kiss For Little Bear* receives *New York Times* Best Illustrated Book Award.

1969 *The Light Princess* receives *New York Times* Best Illustrated Book Award.

1970 *In the Night Kitchen* receives *New York Times* Best Illustrated Book Award; Sendak is awarded the Hans Christian Anderson International Medal by the International Board on Books for Young People.

1971 *In the Night Kitchen* is awardedCaldecott Medal runner-up.

1973 *The Juniper Tree and Other Tales from Grimm* receives *New York Times* Best Illustrated Book Award; *Where the Wild Things Are* and *In the Night Kitchen* receive Art Books for Children Award; *King Grisley-Beard* receives New York Times Best Illustrated Book Award.

1976 *Fly By Night* receives *New York Times* Best Illustrated Book Award.

1981 *Outside Over There* receives *New York Times* Best Illustrated Book Award, *New York Times* Outstanding Book, and *Boston Globe-Horn Book* Award; Sendak is awarded honorary degree from University of Southern Mississippi, Hattiesburg, Mississippi.

1982 *Outside Over There* is awarded Caldecott Medal runner-up.

1983 Sendak is awarded Laura Ingalls Wilder Award, Association for Library Services to Children, for contributions to children's literature.

1984 *The Nutcracker* receives *New York Times* Best Illustrated Book Award; *Where the Wild Things Are* receives *Redbook* Best Young Picture Books Award.

1985 *Where the Wild Things Are* receives Children's Choice Award by the Children's Book Council; *In the Night Kitchen* receives *Redbook* Best Young Picture Books Award.

1985 Sendak is awarded honorary degree from Keene State College, Keene, New Hampshire.

1988 *Where the Wild Things Are* appears on the 100 Books for Reading and Sharing by the New York Public Library.

1996 Sendak is awarded National Medal of the Arts by President Bill Clinton.

1998 Sendak is awarded Visual Arts Award, National Foundation for Jewish Culture.

2003 Sendak is selected May Hill Arbuthnot Honor Lecturer by American Library Association and is the co-winner of the Astrid Lindgren Memorial Award for Literature with Christine Noestlinger, presented by the government of Sweden.

Alderson, Brian. "Children's Books; Children Who Live In Boxes." *The New York Times*, November 14, 1993. *http://query.nytimes.com/gst/fullpage.html?res=9F0CE3D6123AF937 A25752C1A965958260*.

"Artist, Writer and Designer Maurice Sendak." *Fresh Air*, October 30, 2003, *www.npr.org/templates/story/story.php?storyId=1484744*.

Bergstrom, Megan Anderson. "*Dear Mili.*" *Mothering*, Spring 1990, *www.findarticles.com/p/articles/mi_m0838/is_n55/ai_8898303*.

Braun, Saul. "Sendak Raises the Shade on Childhood." *New York Times Sunday Magazine*, June 7, 1970.

Brown, Jennifer M. "The Rumpus Goes On: Max, Maurice Sendak and a Clan of Bears Pay Tribute to a Lifelong Mentorship." *Publishers Weekly*, April 18, 2005.

Capuzzo, Mike. "Sendak's Back, Startling Adults Anew." *Knight-Ridder/Tribune News Service*, September 28, 1993.

Cary, Alice. "Swine Lake: A night at the ballet with Maurice Sendak." Bookpage.com, *www.bookpage.com/9905bp/maurice_sendak.html*.

Davis, David S. "Wrong Recipe Used *In the Night Kitchen.*" *Elementary English*, February 1971, reprinted in Amy Sonheim, *Maurice Sendak.* New York, NY: Twayne Publishers, 1991.

Dooley, Patricia. "*Dear Mili: An Old Tale.*" *School Library Journal*, November 1, 1988.

Evory, Ann, and Linda Metzger, ed., *Contemporary Authors New Revision Series* Vol. 11. Detroit, MI: Gale Research Co., 1984.

Foerstel, Herbert N. *Banned in the USA: A Reference Guide to Book Censorship in Schools and Public Libraries.* Westport, CT: Greenwood Press, 1994.

Gross, Terry. *All I Did Was Ask: Conversations with Writers, Actors, Musicians and Artists.* New York, NY: Hyperion, 2004.

Haas, Susan D. "Maurice Sendak: Forty Years on the Wild Side." *Allentown Morning Call*, September 27, 2003.

Harris, Laurie Lanzen, ed., "Maurice Sendak." *Biography Today Author Series* Vol. 2. Detroit, MI: Omnigraphics Inc., 1996.

Hernandez, Ernio. "Kushner and Sendak's *Brundibar* and *Comedy on the Bridge* Added to Yale Rep Lineup Before NY," *Playbill*, August 31, 2005, *www.playbill.com/news/article/94844.html*.

"Interview with Maurice Sendak," *Backstage at Lincoln Center*, *www.pbs.org/lflc/dec17/sendak.htm*.

Kushner, Tony. *The Art of Maurice Sendak: 1980 to the Present.* New York, NY: Harry N. Abrams Inc., 2003.

Lanes, Selma G. *The Art of Maurice Sendak.* New York, NY: Abradale Press, 1980.

Levine, Judith. *Harmful to Minors.* Minneapolis, MN: University of Minnesota Press, 2002.

Lodge, Sally. "*Brundibar*: A Collaboration with Remarkable Roots." *Publishers Weekly* Vol. 250, No. 43, October 27, 2003.

Maguire, Gregory. "A Sendak Appreciation," *The Horn Book* Vol. 79, No. 6, November 1, 2002.

Marcus, Leonard S. *A Caldecott Celebration: Six Artists and Their Paths to the Caldecott Medal.* New York, NY: Walker and Co., 1998.

Marcus, Leonard S., ed., *Dear Genius: The Letters of Ursula Nordstrom.* New York, NY: HarperCollins, 1999.

"Maurice Sendak Discusses His Work." *Weekend Edition*, National Public Radio, June 4, 2005.

"Maurice Sendak Talks About His New Book, Homelessness." *All Things Considered*, National Public Radio, October 30, 1993.

"The Most Frequently Challenged Books of 2004," American Library Association, *www.ala.org/ala/oif/bannedbooksweek/challengedbanned/challengedbanned.htm*.

NOW with Bill Moyers. *Transcript.* PBS, March 12, 2004, *http://www.pbs.org/now/transcript/transcript311_full.html*

Questions to An Artist Who is Also an Author: A Conversation Between Maurice Sendak and Virginia Haviland. Washington, DC: Library of Congress, 1972.

Reeves, Howard W., ed., *Wings of an Artist: Children's Book Illustrators Talk About Their Art.* New York, NY: Harry N. Abrams Inc., 1999.

Root, Shelton L. "*In the Night Kitchen.*" *Elementary English*, February 1971, reprinted in Amy Sonheim, *Maurice Sendak.* New York, NY: Twayne Publishers, 1991.

Sendak, Maurice. *Higglety Pigglety Pop! or There Must be More to Life.* New York, NY: Harper & Row, 1967.

———. *In the Night Kitchen.* New York: Harper & Row, 1970.

———. "The Nutcracker and the Mouse King," *http://users.htcomp.net/weis/nutcrintro.html*.

———. *Outside Over There.* New York, NY: Harper & Row, 1981.

————. *Where the Wild Things Are*. New York, NY: HarperCollins, 1988.

————. "Why Mickey Wears No Pants." *Los Angeles Times Book Review*, June 16, 1991.

Shirk, Martha. "Gloomy Relatives Inspired 'Wild Things.'" *St. Louis Post-Dispatch*, December 4, 1989, reprinted in Amy Sonheim, *Maurice Sendak* (New York, NY: Twayne Publishers, 1991).

Silver, Judith. "Movie Day at the Supreme Court or 'I Know It When I See It': A History of the Definition of Obscenity." Findlaw.com, *http://library.findlaw.com/2003/May/15/132747.html*.

Smith, Susan Lampert. "A Parental Prerogative . . . Banned Books List Continues to Grow." *Wisconsin State Journal*, September 28, 1993.

Sonheim, Amy. *Maurice Sendak*. New York, NY: Twayne Publishers, 1991.

Spitz, Ellen Handler. *Inside Picture Books*. New Haven, CT: Yale University Press, 1999.

Sutton, Roger. "An Interview with Maurice Sendak." *The Horn Book Magazine* (November–December 2003), *www.hbook.com/publications/magazine/articles/nov03_sendak_sutton.asp*.

Tesoriero, Heather Won. "Where Young Things Are: Maurice Sendak Revives and Lightens a Children's Opera First Performed in a Nazi Concentration Camp." *Time* Vol. 161, No. 22, June 2, 2003.

"Where the Wild Things Roam." *Time* Vol. 142, No. 26, December 20, 1993.

Wright, Sarah H. "Sendak Sketches a Life in Children's Art." Massachusetts Institute of Technology News Office, April 9, 2003, *http://web.mit.edu/newsoffice/2003/sendack-0409.html*.

Zinsser, William, ed., *Worlds of Childhood: The Art and Craft of Writing for Children*. Boston, MA: Houghton Mifflin Co., 1990.

Ackroyd, Peter, Robin Hamlyn, Marilyn Butler, and Michael Phillips, *William Blake*. New York, NY: Harry N. Abrams, 2001.

Arvin, Newton. *Herman Melville*. New York, NY: Grove Press, 2002.

Berg, Julie. *Maurice Sendak*. Minneapolis, MN: Abdo & Daughters, 1993.

Brooks, Philip. *Extraordinary Jewish Americans*. Danbury, CT: Children's Press, 1998.

Denenberg, Barry. *Shadow Life: A Portrait of Anne Frank and Her Family*. New York, NY: Scholastic Press, 2005.

Edwards, Judith. *The Lindbergh Baby Kidnapping in American History*. Berkeley Heights, NJ: Enslow Publishers, 2000.

Fisher, Burton D., ed. *Mozart's Magic Flute*. Coral Gables, FL: Opera Journeys, 2001.

Gay, Peter. *Mozart*. New York, NY: Viking, 1999.

Gaines, Ann. *Maurice Sendak*. Bear, DE: Mitchell Lane Publishers, 2002.

Powers, Bill. *Behind the Scenes of a Broadway Musical*. New York, NY: Crown Publishers, 1982.

Sawyer, Kem Knapp. *Anne Frank*. New York, NY: DK Publishing, 2004.

www.ala.org/ala/oif/bannedbooksweek/challengedbanned/
challengedbanned.htm

Website maintained by the American Library Association (ALA) listing the books that prompt the most requests for censorship. Visitors can review the ALA's strategies for parents, teachers and students to ensure that books are not censored or otherwise removed from library shelves. For example, parents are urged to display the ALA bumper sticker "Book Banning Burns Me Up!" on their cars.

www.pnb.org/season/nutcracker

Pacific Northwest Ballet provides this website to highlight its annual performance of Pyotr Ilyich Tchaikovsky's The Nutcracker. Visitors can read a synopsis of the story as well as a brief history of Maurice Sendak's involvement as set and costume designer.

www.randolphcaldecott.org.uk

The Randolph Caldecott Society of the United Kingdom maintains this website to celebrate the life and work of the 19th-century children's book illustrator who influenced many contemporary artists and writers, including Maurice Sendak. Visitors to the website will find a brief biography of Caldecott as well as examples of his drawings.

www.rosenbach.org/exhibitions/sendakgallery.html

Visitors to the website maintained by the Rosenbach Museum and Library in Philadelphia can find examples of Maurice Sendak's work that are on display in the museum's Sendak Gallery. The website also provides a brief history of the gallery and Sendak's relationship with the museum, which he has chosen to be the repository of much of his notes, sketches and artwork.

HAL MARCOVITZ is a journalist who lives in Pennsylvania with his wife Gail and daughters Ashley and Michelle. He is the author of the novel *Painting the White House* as well as more than seventy nonfiction books for young readers. His other titles in the WHO WROTE THAT? series include biographies of authors Will Hobbs, Bruce Coville, and R.L. Stine.